GUITE TO MODERN THOUGHT

By the same Author

★

Guide to Philosophy
Philosophical Aspects of Modern Science
Return to Philosophy
Matter, Life and Value
Introduction to Modern Philosophy
The Book of Joad: An Autobiography
etc.

C. E. M. JOAD

GUIDE TO MODERN
THOUGHT

FABER AND FABER LIMITED
24 Russell Square
London

First published in January Mcmxxxiii
by Faber and Faber Limited
24 Russell Square, London, W.C.1
Second Impression September Mcmxxxiii
Third Impression January Mcmxxxvi
First reprinted in this edition Mcmxlii
Printed in Great Britain by
Purnell and Sons, Ltd.,
Paulton (Somerset) and London

BOOK
PRODUCTION
WAR ECONOMY
STANDARD

CONTENTS

I. INTRODUCTORY—THE GROUND SURVEYED

II. THE WORLD OF NINETEENTH-CENTURY MATERIALISM

CONTENTS

V. CURRENT THEORIES OF LIFE AND MATTER

CONTENTS

VI. VITALISM AND CREATIVE EVOLUTION

VII. ABNORMAL PSYCHICAL PHENOMENA: SUGGESTED EXPLANATIONS

CONTENTS

I have to thank Professor H. G. Jackson for valuable suggestions in connection with some of the biological passages which occur in Chapter II.

CHAPTER I

INTRODUCTORY—THE GROUND SURVEYED

Questions about the Universe.

This book is concerned not with the facts of science but with their implications. There are certain traditional questions which men and women have asked in all ages, and which they are still asking to-day. Is the universe a fortuitous collocation of atoms, or is it the embodiment of design and plan? Is the world we know a chance world, or a planned? Is life an incidental by-product of material processes, a mere eddy in the primaeval slime, or is it fundamental in the scheme of things? Is the process of evolution haphazard or purposive? Is humanity, in particular, its most promising achievement, destined to carry life to higher levels than have yet appeared, or is it doomed to failure and extinction so soon as the material conditions which favoured its development have ceased to obtain? Are we free to make our lives as we please, or are our wills determined by bodily reflexes and unconscious wishes? Is mind a unique and independent activity, or a mere function of bodily processes which have produced consciousness as a kind of glow surrounding the brain like the bright colours on an oil-film?

The examination of these questions belongs to philosophy, and, although no philosopher has been able satisfactorily to settle them—it is doubtful, indeed, whether they are capable of settlement—philosophers have been able to suggest fruitful hypotheses by way of answer, and to give reasons which have seemed to many convincing in support of these hypotheses.

To assist him in formulating his hypothesis (which he has usually called not a hypothesis at all, but a philosophy, or a system, or a theory of the universe) the philosopher takes into account all branches and aspects of human knowledge and experience. The inspiration of the artist, the vision of the mystic, the social urge of the reformer, the emotions of the lover, and the moral intuitions of the plain man, all are grist to the philosopher's mill. He must also take into consideration the conclusions and discoveries of the scientist.

The scientist, working away in his own special compartment, devotes his attention to a certain carefully delimited section of the universe. Thus enclosed, he arrives at more or less definite conclusions without stopping to consider what relation they bear to the conclusions reached by other scientists working in their watertight compartments. This is not a criticism of the scientist; cosmic correlation is not his business, but it is not to be wondered at if some of the conclusions clash. Hence arises the need for a clearing-house in which the results arrived at by the various sciences can be pooled and collated, in order that, looking at them as a whole, we may be able to infer what kind of universe it is that we live in, and hazard a guess at the destiny of human life within it.

Reports from the Sciences.

Of recent years these 'results' from the special sciences have tended to transcend in importance the other types of data which have historically formed the raw material of philosophy. People's moral intuitions have for years remained fairly constant; recently they seemed to have diminished both in frequency and in intensity; mystics have been few; there are still great artists, but the problems which their art raises are not in any sense new, while there is no reason to think that the lover of to-day experiences very different emotions from his predecessors in Shakespeare's England or Renaissance Florence. But the sciences have been advancing at a prodigious rate and presenting the philosophers with data faster than they can assimilate them.

The discovery of evolution, for example, necessitated

the consideration of the whole question of purpose and design from a fresh angle and in relation to new evidence; it also raised difficult and intriguing problems with regard to the nature of life and time. The Russian psychologist Pavlov's experiments on conditioned reflexes have thrown a new light upon the relation of the mind to the body and necessitated a reconsideration of the question of free will. But it is from the physical sciences that the stream of new facts comes fastest. During the last thirty years our conceptions of the physical world have been revolutionised. The theories of relativity, special and general, have altered our views of the nature of space and time, while the quantum theory has necessitated a new conception of the nature of matter and energy. Impelled by this theory or, rather, by its surprising implications, physicists are presenting us with new pictures of the atom, the fundamental constituent of matter, at the rate of one every four or five years. They are finding, moreover, that their researches increasingly take them into territory which has traditionally belonged to philosophy. Unable to carry the analysis of matter further without raising philosophical problems, physicists show a tendency to do their philosophising for themselves. Inadvisedly, as one cannot but feel, for the philosophising of the physicists is noticeably inferior to their physics, and eminent men are at the moment engaged in making all the mistakes which the philosophers made for themselves some three hundred years ago and have been engaged in detecting and correcting ever since. In particular it is thought that modern physics lends support to Idealism, and suggests, if it does not actually require, a religious interpretation of the universe.

Decline of Materialism.

This rather unexpected result has come about in the following way. Nineteenth-century physics was essentially materialistic. Under its influence physicists until recent years have been dominated by the notion that to be real a thing must be of the same nature as a piece of matter.

Matter was something lying out there in space. It was hard, simple and obvious; indubitably it was real, and as such calculated to form an admirable foundation upon which the horse sense of the practical man could base his irrefragable convictions. Now matter was something which one could see and touch. It followed that whatever else was real must be of the same nature as that which one could theoretically see and touch. Hence, to enquire into the nature of the things we saw and touched, to analyse them into their elements and atoms, was to deal directly with reality: to apprehend values or to enjoy religious experience was to wander in a world of shadows. Common sense, under the influence of science, took the same view; to use the eye of the body to view the physical world, was to acquaint oneself with what was real; to use that of the soul to see visions was to become the victim of illusion. And the views of the universe to which the visions led had, it was urged, no objective reality. Common sense generally embodies the petrified science of fifty years ago, and most of us to-day, except on Sundays —when our belief is qualified by a conventional but intermittent admission of the reality of the spiritual—instinctively assume that only material things are real. Parallel with this belief that the real must be a substance tangible and visible was the belief that it must be subject to the laws which were observed to operate in the physical world —that it must work, in short, like a machine. As Professor Eddington puts it, nineteenth-century science was disposed, as soon as it scented a piece of mechanism, to exclaim, 'Here we are getting to bedrock. This is what things should resolve themselves into. This is ultimate reality'.[1] The implication was that whatever did not show itself amenable to mechanistic causation—value, for example, or the feeling of moral obligation, or the sense of deity—was not quite real.

To-day the foundation for this whole way of thinking, the hard, obvious, simple lumps of matter, has disappeared.

[1] Eddington. *Science and the Unseen World*, p. 21.

Modern matter is something infinitely attenuated and elusive; it is a hump in space time, a 'mush' of electricity, a wave of probability undulating into nothingness; frequently it turns out not to be matter at all but a projection of the consciousness of its perceiver. So mysterious, indeed, has it become, that the modern tendency to explain things in terms of mind is little more than a preference for explanation in terms of the less unknown rather than of the more.

Science, Religion and Philosophy.

The imaginative conception of reality no longer being limited by likeness to the things we can see or touch, there is room for wider views. Value, for example, may be real, and so may be the objects of the ethical and the religious consciousness. Hence, there is now no need for those who accept the results of the physical sciences to write off, as they had once to write off, as subjective illusions the promptings of the moral and the aesthetic sides of their natures, and the nineteenth-century gulf between science and religion is in a fair way to being bridged.

This is not to say that physical science supports, still less that it proves religion, although many, including some of those whose views I propose to examine, seem to think that it does. The only conclusion we are justified in drawing is the negative one that the reasons which physical science was formerly thought to provide for supposing that religion was necessarily false no longer obtain, and the way is, therefore, open for a reconsideration of the religious interpretation of the universe on merits.

The immediate effect of the new situation is that physicists seem to feel a growing need to travel outside the bounds of physics in quest of a solution of the problems that physics raises. Philosophy being demanded, a number of physicists, as I have already pointed out, are doing their philosophising for themselves and surmise that behind the world which physics studies there is another. This other world is conceived as a mental or spiritual unity; matter, it is said, is only its appearance, whence it is but a step to the announcement that mind alone is real and matter is its creature, which modern physicists make as cheerfully and almost as dogmatically as their materialist predecessors announced fifty years ago that matter alone was real and that mind was an unimportant emanation of matter.

From the other side philosophers are increasingly concerning themselves with the problems set by physics. But, whether it is by physicists turned philosophers or by philosophers who find themselves compelled to take cognisance of the conclusions of physics, the traditional questions of the nature and constitution of the universe and the meaning and status of life are being viewed from a new angle, and canvassed in the light of fresh evidence.

Evolution as a Creative Process.

Nor is it only the physical sciences which are demanding philosophical interpretation. The mechanist theory which proclaimed life a by-product of non-living processes and mind an offshoot of the brain is proving increasingly unsatisfactory in biology. From a number of quarters evidence is accumulating to suggest that the mode of behaviour of a living organism is fundamentally different from that of a machine and can never be explained in terms of it. Life, it seems, is fundamental; moreover, it is creative and uses and moulds the forms of living organisms as instruments to further its purposes and serve its ends. Hence arise theories of creative evolution which interpret evolution as the expression of a purposive force or principle which, manifesting itself in living organisms, seeks to achieve ever higher qualities of life in the effort to realise some objective at which we can at present only dimly guess.

Even those who do not go so far as to postulate a special activity or stream of life which uses matter as its instrument, who, indeed, refuse to accept the distinction between life and matter, mind and body, as fundamental, are no longer content with materialism; and theories of emergent evolution, of 'organism', and of what is known as 'holism', have taken the place of the nineteenth-century view which, diminishingly held as a theory of the universe, subsides into the position of a useful postulate or assumption for the guidance of laboratory workers. These conduct their researches—they must, indeed, so conduct them, for they have no alternative—*as if* mechanism were true, and every cause produced its determined and predictable effect. But, when we come to interpretation, other conceptions are introduced, and there seems to be a growing consensus of opinion in favour of what are called organic or even vitalist views. Evolution, in other words, is coming to be regarded as a creative process, continually engaged in bringing to birth something new; there is literally more in the universe at any moment than there was the moment before; the future is unpredictable and man is free within limits to make it as he pleases.

Mechanist views in Psychology.

But, while physics leans increasingly to a spiritual interpretation and biology stresses creativity and purpose, psychology has moved in the other direction. Much modern psychology is thoroughly determinist in outlook; it tends to throw doubt upon the uniqueness of man's mind and to deny the freedom of his will.

This result comes about in two different ways; there are, that is to say, two distinct branches of this very confused science which reach what are in effect the same answers to most of the questions formulated on the first page, by different routes. In the first place, Behaviourism has achieved unexpected success in interpreting the behaviour of human beings without introducing the assumption that they have minds. They may have, of course, for, since a mind cannot be observed, to deny it is, it is held, as unreasonable as to assert it; but, if they have, there is no reason to think that their minds influence their behaviour.

Behaviourism.

This, at least, is the assertion of the Behaviourists. Beginning with a study of animal psychology, they reached certain conclusions tending to show that animals were automata. These conclusions nobody felt impelled to resist, since few supposed that animals were virtuous and fewer still had any interest in maintaining that they possessed minds. The Behaviourists then proceeded to apply their conclusions to human beings, who were humiliated to find how mindless they could be made to appear, but were, nevertheless, unable to produce very convincing reasons for supposing that they were not the highly complicated automata which the Behaviourists represented them to be. Pavlov's celebrated study of the conditioned reflexes of dogs made our automatism more credible by showing how and why simple physical stimuli could produce such catastrophic and apparently irrelevant responses, as when the receipt of a sheet of paper bearing the imprint of a black hand causes the victim in a boys' crook story to go and throw himself over the edge of a cliff. A difficult proposition, one would have supposed, to explain the suicide response to the black-hand stimulus without supposing that the victim had a mind which grasped the *import*, the *significance*, of the black hand; but Pavlov's work enables us to see how it can be done without assuming that the victim is anything but body. It is, indeed, precisely this assumption that human beings are *all* body and *only* body that the Behaviourists have very ably advocated and, if it could be successfully maintained, it would, it is obvious, imply a very different set of answers to our fundamental questions than those which physics and biology are inclined to suggest.

Psycho-Analysis.

In the second place, the theories of psycho-analysts, while not casting doubt about the existence of mind, clearly demonstrate the dependence of its rational upon its non-rational elements. Consciousness, they maintain, is for the most part nothing but a screen put up by the unconscious to save our *amour propre*; conscious events are the distorted reflections of unconscious desires and impulses, and what we think, feel and do is determined not *by* us but *for* us by forces deep down in the recesses of our personalities, whose genesis escapes detection and whose workings evade control.

Modern psychology proper, while rejecting the somewhat bizarre machinery of psycho-analysis, issues in the works of many writers in not dissimilar conclusions. It is, that is to say, fundamentally irrationalist in tendency, sees in instinct and impulse the mainspring of our personalities and exhibits reason and will as mere corks bobbing on the waves of desire.

Thus reason is the handmaid of our instincts, not the arbiter of our destinies; its function is to provide us with justifications for what we instinctively wish to believe and pretexts for what we instinctively want to do, while the will is no less enslaved to elements in our natures which we do not control and for which we cannot be held responsible.

If we are not ultimately responsible for what we think or what we do, if our natures are formed not *by* us but *for* us, free will, it is clear, is a delusion. We are automata no less on the psycho-analyst view than on the behaviourist; we are determined, it is true, not by our bodily responses to external stimuli, but by instinctive trends of which we are unconscious; but we are determined none the less for that.

Thus the implications of contemporary psychology, in so far as it is represented by the two important schools of thought at which I have glanced, run counter to those of physics and biology. Mind, it seems, is not unique; freedom is an illusion; ethics is a rationalisation of non-ethical impulses; purpose and design are figments; living organisms are no less automata than machines. These, at least, are the conclusions suggested by Behaviourism and psycho-analysis, the two most distinctive schools of modern psychology.

Summary.

It will be seen, from this brief summary, that the implications of modern science are far from clear. They are, in fact, exceedingly confused; different sciences point in different directions and the reports which reach us from the students in one branch of enquiry contradict those which come from another. In particular, while physics and, to some extent, biology are thought to point in the direction of an idealist interpretation of the universe, an interpretation which does not exclude the notions of purpose and design, the tendency of psychology is to suggest a chance world of happenings whose fundamental analysis is in terms of mindless events. The schools of modern psychology to which I have referred nowhere imply that will and reason are free, or that mind is fundamental and bears witness to something fundamentally akin to itself at the heart of things; they suggest, in fact, precisely the contrary —that mind is an unplanned accident in the universe and that the alien and the brutal condition and determine what is spiritual and akin.

Not less interesting than the implications of the sciences themselves is their effect upon contemporary thought. This, as might be expected, is as confused as the intellectual background from which it springs. There is a certain vague consciousness of the fact that materialism is losing ground, and that the closed circle of the mechanist universe of the nineteenth century has been broken; but there is no clear conception of what has come to take its place. Materialism was like a frost; it held the scheme of things fast bound in the laws of an iron determinism. The frost has broken up, but with the thaw there has set in a general deliquescence of thought in which the old boundaries and signposts have disappeared. The present position is distinguished by two outstanding characteristics, neither of which contributes to ease of comprehension.

Sense of New Beginnings.

In the first place, there is a general sense of new beginnings such as, I imagine, must have been felt at the time of the Renaissance. The nineteenth-century view seems to have been that we were within reasonable distance of attaining a complete understanding of man and the universe. It is only now that we are coming to realise our comparative ignorance of both. Most of the knowledge previously obtained is seen to be misleading and, where the old methods have failed, there is a willingness to experiment with new ones. The nineteenth century regarded European civilisation as mature and late, the final expression of the human spirit;[1] we are only now beginning to realise that it is young and childish. The race, it seems, is still in its infancy, and what has hitherto been achieved is little more than the advance from crawling to the first few hesitant steps that prelude rather than *are* walking.

This sense of new beginnings is characteristic not only of contemporary science but of contemporary art. In art, as in science, there is a tendency to break with past traditions and to experiment with new methods. The interest of the contemporary artist lies less in the achievements of the past than in the possibilities of the future; he experiments with new methods in the hope of realising these possibilities. It is this interest in the future that constitutes one of our chief differences from our predecessors. The nineteenth century believed in progress, yet, believing also that it knew the main lines upon which progress would proceed, it was little interested in what was to come. On the whole it looked backward rather than forward. Men felt that they had travelled a long way to become what they were, and the journey, its main difficulties already passed, interested them as perils overcome will interest men within striking distance of their goal.

[1] See *Victoriana* compiled by Margaret Barton and Osbert Sitwell (practically any extract).

Hence, their concern with the future was limited to fore-casting the development of machines and speculations such as are to be found in the early romantic novels of H. G. Wells. We have discovered that the journey was even longer and more perilous than the nineteenth century supposed, yet we know ourselves to be still at its very beginning. Hence our interest in what is to come, which expresses itself in a constant stream of books and pamph-lets on every possible aspect of the future, ranging from the 'Future of Clothes' to the 'Future of Physics', and from the 'Future of Apron Strings'[1] to the 'Future of Humour'. Now this looking forward is, I suggest, an out-come of the felt uncertainties of the present. We have come, we feel, to a definite break in the tradition of our civilisation. The nineteenth century was the end of an epoch; we, it is increasingly evident, are at the beginning of another.

Scepticism and Humility.

In the second place, modern thought is characterised by a scepticism as to its conclusions and a freedom in its use of hypotheses. The modern universe is more mys-terious and elusive than the world of the nineteenth cen-tury. The area of what is known being diminished, the field of what is possible is correspondingly enlarged. Not only is there scepticism as to the conclusions reached, but doubt as to the proper methods of reaching them. Hence, men are not only more willing to explore different avenues of possible understanding of the universe, art as well as science, religious ecstasy as well as common sense, but within the boundaries of science itself they are continually trying new instruments. As Sir William Bragg says, 'We use the classical theory on Mondays, Wednesdays and Fridays, and the quantum theory on Tuesdays, Thursdays and Saturdays.'[2]

On reflection this new humility with regard both to

---

[1] A volume recently announced in the 'To-day and To-morrow Series'.
[2] Quoted by Whetham. *History of Science*, p. 485.

methods and conclusions is seen to be inevitable. The more we enlarge the sphere of the known the more, it is obvious, we enlarge its area of contact with the unknown, and in so doing we realise our ignorance.

A similar position is being reached from the side of religion, where scepticism with regard to the traditional creeds is combined with a growing interest in the religious view of the world and a conviction that science has not necessarily said the last word.

The resultant scepticism and fluidity of thought are natural enough in the circumstances; but they do not make things easy for the enquirer who wants to know precisely what the modern universe is supposed to be like.

Irrationalism.

While, however, the influence of physics has bewildered people's minds and left them confused and uncertain, the influence of modern psycho-analysis is as widespread as its import is clear. Freud's writings are considerably read, and the belief in the importance of the unconscious is common to people of widely different outlooks. The influence of this belief is profound. It issues in practice in a distrust of reason, a tendency to probe beneath the surface and a conviction that the motives which determine men's conduct are rarely such as they profess. This is not to accuse people of hypocrisy—it is not suggested that they are themselves aware of why they do what they do—it is merely to throw doubt on the front of apparent rationality and self-control which they exhibit to the world. These things are, it seems, a mask rather than a face.

The resultant irrationalism, if I may so term it, pervades every department of modern intellectual activity, notably politics and literature; in politics it is responsible for a growing distrust of democracy and in literature for the vogue of the psychological novel.

Purpose of Book.

It will be my object in this book to disentangle, so far as I can, this tangled skein of modern thought. I shall try to describe in turn the views which are current to-day in physics, biology and psychology, to give the reasons for them and briefly to trace their implications. Assuming the truth of the conclusions reached by these three sciences, my main concern throughout will be to consider what answers they entitle us to give to the general questions asked on the first page. I shall also endeavour to estimate the influence upon contemporary thought of some of the theories discussed.

The treatment of the various issues raised will be popular throughout. I shall avoid technical terms and assume in the reader no previous acquaintance with the subjects under discussion. The task is far from easy; nevertheless, I believe that it is possible without being unduly abstruse to convey some idea of the general trends of modern thought and the conclusions to which the various branches of it seem to point. I shall begin with a preliminary chapter on nineteenth-century materialism from the break-up of which most of the theories with which I shall be concerned take their rise.

CHAPTER II

THE WORLD OF NINETEENTH-CENTURY MATERIALISM

Nature and Tenets of Materialism.

In the nineteenth century the cumulative effect of the discoveries which had been made during the preceding three hundred years enabled man to do what in his long history he had never done before, namely, to formulate a general theory of the universe. This theory, based on the mechanics of Galileo and Newton, pictured the universe as a vast machine and explained everything that happened in it in terms of the movements of pieces of matter. The explanation applied not only to all events that did happen but to all that could happen, since any kind of event other than the movements of matter was, in the dominant contemporary scientific view, regarded as inconceivable. Owing to its experimental triumphs this hypothesis led increasing numbers of thoughtful people to accept materialism as a philosophy of life. Even to-day most people hold instinctively that to be real is to be material and unconsciously assume that, whereas two apples may be found in the world outside themselves, the number two itself exists only in their minds.

But in spite of its experimental successes materialism suffered from one great defect: it took from man his significance in the cosmic scheme of things and denied reality to his mind. This would not have mattered—there is, after all, no particular reason why the universe should have been designed to give man significance—but for the unfortunate fact that materialism itself was a product of man's mind. If the latter was fictitious, then the philosophy which proclaimed it to be so was itself a figment. However, it is not my purpose in this chapter to attempt to criticise materialism, but to explain, as briefly as I can,

27

what the doctrine in its nineteenth-century form asserted, and to give a brief account of the considerations which led men to adopt it.

What Darwin discovered.

The evidence for materialism was derived mainly from three sources, namely, biology, psychology and physics. I will consider the biological source first. The discoveries of Darwin were thought to show that the evolution of life from its earliest beginnings to its most elaborate product, the mind of the nineteenth-century scientist, could be interpreted as the result of the occurrence of small variations in species, reacting to material forces and developing according to ascertained laws.

Life, it was found, had evolved, by a gradual yet continuous process, from the earliest forms of living organisms up to its latest and most elaborate product, man. The earliest forms of life were thought to have appeared as specks of protoplasmic jelly in the scum left by the tides as they receded from the shores of the world's first seas. In the warm waters of the proterozoic seas anything from six hundred to sixty million years ago, there were amoebas and there were jelly fish; the earth grew cooler, life left the waters and proliferated into enormous reptile-like creatures, the dinosaurs and gigantosaurs of the mesozoic age; cooler still, and there were birds and mammals. Among them was a smaller lemur-like creature, a comparatively late comer whose descendants split into two branches; the one developed into the anthropoid apes, the other culminated in man.

Such was the process which Darwin envisaged, the process of the evolution of life as a consequence of the operation of purely natural forces. Man, the most conceited of the mammals, could only recover from the shock of learning of his relationship to the lower animals by representing the process as a progress; if he was later than the amoeba, then, he affirmed, he must also be higher. Whether the amoeba would agree with this opinion is not known, and, until we are in a position to obtain the amoeba's views, we should do well to suspend judgment. But there is nothing of this in Darwin. Refraining from moralising the process of evolution into a progress, he was content to discover the process and modern biology has done little more than dot the i's and cross the t's of his discovery.

Natural Selection.

The modifications which it has been found necessary to introduce into Darwin's account of evolution are, indeed, surprisingly few. One of them is concerned with the way in which changes in species resulting in new species arise. Darwin thought that these changes were due to the accumulation of minute variations. That variations do occur is obvious, since, if all offspring entirely resembled their parents, the world would still be populated by amoebas and jelly fish. As it is not, we must suppose that to certain creatures there were born offspring that exhibited certain differences from their parents. These differences would be of two kinds: either they would assist the creature in the struggle for existence, or they would handicap it. If they assisted it, the creature would secure a larger share of the available food, would prosper accordingly, choose a well-nourished mate exhibiting a similar variation, and produce offspring in which the original difference was reproduced and intensified: thus a new species gradually came into being. If they did not, the creature would be eliminated and its unsuccessful variation would be eliminated with it. The origin of new species was thus, in Darwin's view, due to the appearance of variations which have what is called a survival value. Hence, the importance of the two Darwinian principles, 'natural selection' and 'the survival of the fittest'. The food supply is conceived to be limited and the members of a particular species struggle for it. Those who exhibit a variation of a kind likely to be serviceable in the struggle, fleetness of foot, for instance, or strength of muscle, or length of neck, will tend to have an advantage over their fellows. In virtue of their superior 'fitness' they will accordingly tend to survive while their rivals are eliminated. Thus by a process of automatic sifting out, nature 'selects' those who, in virtue of the variations which they embody, possess an advantage in the struggle for existence.

Now Darwin conceived these 'variations' as small modifications appearing by chance, and becoming gradually more marked in each generation in which they appeared. Ultimately, under the influence of natural selection they would become so pronounced as to constitute what would in effect amount to a new species. Thus new species developed out of older ones as the result of the gradual accumulation of chance minute variations.

Since Darwin's death the theory of natural selection has been modified in one important respect. The modification is entailed by a distinction which has been introduced between two sorts of variations, termed respectively 'individual fluctuations' and 'mutations'. Most of the variations which occur in offspring are now known as 'individual fluctuations'. These are such as may be found in any litter of animals, and are caused by environmental influences. They are not transmitted to offspring and are, therefore, of very little importance from the evolutionary point of view. A 'mutation' entails a fundamental and continuing alteration in the heredity of the creature and proceeds from a change in the germ plasm itself. In virtue of this change, the germ plasm of the offspring differs from that of the parent and originates the character or characters whose appearance in the offspring constitutes the 'mutation'. If they pass the sieve of natural selection, this character or these characters will continue to appear in future generations, whatever the conditions in which the species develops, and may constitute the starting-point of a new species which establishes itself either to the exclusion of the old one or side by side with it.

But the introduction of this distinction and the substitution of 'mutations' arising from changes in the germ plasm for Darwin's variations throw no light upon the question: 'What is the cause of variations?' We have simply to substitute the question: 'What is the cause of those variations which are "mutations"?'

The cause of variations? Importance of the question.

It is from the answer which was given to this question that materialism on its biological side took its rise. The importance of the question is obvious. It is by means of variations that living species change, new species arise, evolution advances and, in the course of its advance, produces man. Man himself is, in fact, simply a variation, or rather the result of a series of variations. Hence, to know the cause of variations is to know not only the motive force of evolution; it is to know the origin of ourselves. To this question Darwin gave no answer. As to the cause of variations he prudently professed ignorance; to be precise, he ascribed them to chance. The importance of this view of evolution lies in the fact that, *given the variations*, the activity of no external force or agency, mind, spirit, God, call it what you will, need be invoked, no prearranged plan or purpose assumed in order to explain the history of life on the earth. The facts may be adequately explained by the inevitable workings of natural law.

The only other view in the field was that of the followers of the French biologist Lamarck. Lamarck had maintained that variations in species resulted from the efforts of individuals to fit themselves into a changing environment by forming new habits adapted to the environment. New habits would involve a new use for certain organs, while other organs would tend to fall into disuse. Thus the new habit gradually induced a change in the physical characteristics of the creature, this change entailing a gain in some qualities and a loss in respect of others, and, Lamarck's followers held, being in some degree transmitted to the creature's offspring. Thus the continuous and energetic use of its neck by the giraffe stretching to reach high branches, of his arms by the blacksmith continuously lifting heavy weights, and of its toes by the horse raising itself upon them to achieve a yet greater speed, will develop neck, arms and toes during the lifetimes of giraffe, blacksmith and horse. Conversely the disuse of any organ—for example, the disuse of certain limbs in snakes and lizards and whales and of tails in apes—will lead to an atrophy of the organ in question. Lamarck's formula was, then, that new characters acquired by use, disuse or habit, will be handed on to future generations. But while Lamarck held that it was the *conscious* effort of the organism to adapt itself that produced the change, his followers tended increasingly to regard it as evoked *unconsciously*. Their formula was slightly different from that of Lamarck. For them the origin of the whole process was change in the environment; the creature either adapted itself to the change, or it did not. If it did, it varied in respect of the adaptation and the variation was transmitted. If it did not, it perished in the struggle for existence.

Now both Darwin's view and Lamarck's issue in one very important conclusion. It is agreed that variations in species are the cause of all the changes that separate man from the amoeba; in them is to be found the key to the development of life, and the origin of the appearance of human beings. It is because of the variations that mind has evolved, that man is able to grapple with relativity, to compose symphonies and to commune with God. Yet when we ask what causes the variations, Darwin replies 'an accident', and Lamarck's followers 'the influence of the material environment'. Thus the appearance and evolution of life are explained without the introduction of any vital principle or mental concept; there is no purpose that life fulfils, no plan that it embodies.

The behaviour of living things is to be interpreted exclusively in terms of their reactions to their environment and, in order to explain the developments which began with the amoeba and culminated in man, it is necessary merely to understand the laws in accordance with which living organisms react to their environment.[1]

Thus the materialist interpretation of biology pre-supposes that causation proceeds always from the less developed to the more, from the non-living to the living, from environment to body and from body to mind. But is this last link in the materialist chain, the step from body to mind, justified?

Body-Mind Problem.

For at this point the question may well be asked, 'What about mind? Mind assuredly is not material and, so far from being determined by matter, can in some degree control it. If, for example, I *will* to chisel a lump of stone into the shape of a human head, am I not freely altering my environment to please myself? Can it in any sense be maintained that I am merely adapting myself to or re-acting to my environment?'

The answer to this question was provided by nineteenth-century psychology, which constituted the second main source of the materialist philosophy. In order to realise the significance and plausibility of the answer, let us consider for a moment the astonishing fact of the mind-body relationship. That mind and body are continually interacting is obvious. If I get drunk, I see double; if I take a late supper of cold pork and pickles, I have a night-mare and dream about blue devils; if I inhale nitrous-oxide gas, I experience an ecstatic vision in which I find myself in Paradise enjoying the converse of God and His angels. These are instances of the influence of the body upon the mind.

If I see a ghost, my hair stands on end; if I am to address a public meeting, I sweat; if I see a cricket ball coming, I hold out my hands or flinch and duck, as the case may be. These are instances of the influence of the mind on the body. Examples could be multiplied indefinitely, the inter-action of mind and body being a fact which is testified by

[1] This is precisely what modern psychology seeks to do (see Chapter III).

every moment of our waking lives. Yet, when we come to reflect upon it, how odd a fact it is.

The body is a piece of matter; as such it possesses the properties of matter, weight, mass, shape, size and so forth, and obeys the laws of physics. The mind we conceive to be different; it is, we say, immaterial; it has, therefore, neither weight, mass, nor size; it does not occupy space and it does not obey the laws of physics. How, then, if mind and matter are so different that they have not a single quality in common, can they influence one another? How indeed can they 'get at' one another at all? A paving-stone can crush a butterfly because the butterfly, like itself, possesses mass and substance; but how can it affect a wish? The length of the arm can be measured, but who can measure the inspiration which went to the composition of Beethoven's Fifth Symphony?

It is no exaggeration to say that this fundamental problem is one which all psychology must attempt to solve and no psychology has yet satisfactorily solved.

The two clocks.

The attempts at solution begin as early as the seventeenth century, when Descartes formulated the theory which has served as the starting point for most subsequent discussions of the subject. The newly discovered science of mechanics had shown that the movements of matter were determined and could be calculated in accordance with known laws. Now the body was a piece of matter. Therefore it seemed that the movements of the body were determined; and, indeed, it is the case that, if I and a large stone are dropped over a precipice, my behaviour will be determined by precisely the same laws as those which govern the behaviour of the stone. This result was distasteful to philosophers who wished to believe that, so far as their minds at any rate were concerned, they were free. The only way of reconciling their wishes with mechanics seemed to be to proclaim that the mind was independent of and therefore not determined by the movements of the body. Mind, it was insisted, was one thing, body another; and neither could influence the other. How then account for the fact of their apparent continual interaction? Descartes's answer[1] was to the effect that mind and body proceeded, as it were, on parallel lines—parallel, because parallel lines were at that time thought not to meet and, therefore, suggested the requisite notion of non-interaction. Nevertheless, every event in the one was accompanied by a corresponding event in the other. This invariable accompaniment of mental events by bodily, and bodily by mental, was not the result, as might have been supposed, of the existence of a causal relation—it was not the case that event x in the body *caused* idea y, or vice versa—since this would have re-introduced the notion of interaction, but was due to the benevolence of the deity, who, in order that man might live and function, had so arranged matters that the feeling of hunger should be accompanied by (without causing) the movement of the hand containing food to the mouth.

A simile often invoked to illustrate this conception is that of two perfectly synchronised clocks. The tick of each is accompanied by the tick of the other, not because the one tick *causes* the other, but because they have been wound and set together. Similarly mind and body had been initially wound and set and were now kept going by the creator, and their apparent interaction was a witness to an indefinitely repeated series of divine miracles, which secured that every event in the one was accompanied by an appropriate event in the other.

Epiphenomenal View of Mind.

It was not to be expected that this theory, later known as psycho-physical parallelism, with its resort to a perpetually intruding *deus ex machina*, would be accepted by

---

[1] More precisely, the answer was that of Descartes's successors, known as Occasionalists. Descartes's own doctrine is confused and not always consistent. He maintains, for example, that interaction of a modified kind *does* take place in the pineal gland, which was supposed to be situated at the centre of the brain.

nineteenth-century science. Scientists were sceptical of the existence, rationalists threw doubt upon the benevolence of God, and the hypothesis of continuous divine intervention was in due course abandoned. Since, if the body and mind are radically different, their interaction is a mystery, and, since science is impatient of mysteries, it was inferred that they could not be really different. Now, the body is undoubtedly material; therefore the mind must, it was urged, be material too. In the infinite permutations and combinations through which the forms of matter have passed since the universe began, matter has, it was suggested, achieved a form in which it has become conscious of itself. The consciousness of matter by itself is called mind. Mind, then, is matter of a very refined and attenuated type; it was conceived as a sort of glow surrounding the brain rather like the halo round the head of the saint, and the function of the halo was to reflect the events which occur in the brain.

When I touch a red-hot poker, a stimulus is applied at the ends of my fingers; this stimulus constitutes a message which travels along the nerves running up my arm and ultimately reaches the brain. Here it causes a set of disturbances among the highly complicated layers of nerves of which the brain is composed. The glow of consciousness lights up these disturbances with the result that I am said to know or to feel the heat of the poker, the knowing or feeling being what is called a mental event. From this conclusion there follows a highly important consequence. If the function of the mind is confined to lighting up or reflecting the events that occur in the brain, it cannot, it is clear, reflect what is not there. Hence nothing can happen in the mind unless it has first happened in the brain, that is to say, in the body, and all mental events are preceded and caused by bodily events.

Thus we reach the so-called epiphenomenal theory of mind. Mind is a by-product of the functioning of material processes, those, namely, which occur in the body. It does not initiate events on its own account, and free will is, therefore, an illusion; it merely reflects bodily happenings which are themselves responses to external stimuli. It illuminates these happenings when they reach the brain in the form of cerebral events, and, illuminating them, becomes aware of them; but from the very nature of things it cannot cause them. From the nature of things it cannot illuminate what is not there. Therefore, its activity and contents are entirely determined by what is there. Hence, if the existence of mind is admitted at all, it is regarded as a helpless spectator of the drama of the body, a spectator who is no more responsible for the events he witnesses than is the audience for the play.

I shall consider some of the implications and recent developments of this view of mind in the next chapter.

Nineteenth-Century Physics.

Of the third source of the materialist philosophy, nineteenth-century physics, very little need be said. I have already referred to the contemporary view of matter, abandoned only in the present century, which represented it as something hard, solid and tangible, the nature of which was vouchsafed by a kind of revelation to the mind of the investigating scientist exactly as it was. Matter so conceived became at once the model and the touchstone of reality. Not only was matter real but whatever else was real must, it was thought, be of the same nature as matter: if reality consisted of, and only of, matter, every phenomenon actual and conceivable must be due to the movements of matter, since there was nothing else to move.

Matter was thought to consist of atoms which, hard, indestructible, and homogeneous, formed the very bedrock of reality. The movements of the atom were, it was believed, determined by the laws of mechanics and dynamics. These laws were absolute, and all other laws were derived from them. Thus materialism explained everything in terms of the different arrangements and combinations of material particles. Little lumps of material, moving in space according to necessary and inevitable laws, have produced our hopes, our fears, the scent of the rose, the colours of the sunset, and the mystic's experience of God. They have also produced our knowledge of the little bits; mind, in short, is merely the consciousness by the bits of themselves.

I shall, in the fourth chapter, criticise this conception, and show how in modern physics it has been to a large extent abandoned.

Materialist Conception of the Universe.

Combining the conclusions of nineteenth-century biology, nineteenth-century psychology and nineteenth-century physics, we obtain the following result. All mental events are caused by preceding cerebral events; all cerebral events are subject to the law of cause and effect, and are caused, therefore, by preceding bodily events or by external stimuli to which they are responses; the preceding bodily events are in their turn caused either by preceding bodily events or by external stimuli. Along these lines we travel backward until we reach the first events in the history of the organism, which are the result of its initial inheritance or of its external environment. In so far as they are the result of inheritance, they can be traced back to the variations which made the creature what it is. These variations are themselves either chance happenings or the result of the action of external environment. The chain of causation from a happening in the external world to a thought in the mind is, therefore, complete; at every stage the material conditions and precedes the vital, and we have only to learn enough about the laws of matter to be able to describe and predict any and every event that has occurred or can occur in the history of the universe. Professor Tyndall, speaking at a meeting of the British Association in 1874, grandiosely summed up the position when he prophesied that science would one day be able to envisage and to explain all that has happened and does happen in terms of the 'ultimately purely natural and inevitable march of evolution from the atoms of the primaeval nebula to the proceedings of the British Association for the Advancement of Science'.

Unimportance of Life.

It will be readily apparent how adversely this view reflects upon man's natural belief in the special significance of life in general, of human life in particular, and of the most important expression of human life—mind. Copernicus abolished the primacy of man's planet in the universe, Darwin abolished the primacy of man within his planet, and materialistic psychology abolished the primacy of mind within the man. To the general disparagement of the importance of life initiated by biology and psychology, geology and astronomy were only too ready to contribute. Geology had enormously extended the age of the world, astronomy the size and spread of space; there were vast epochs when it was practically certain that the earth was without life; there were millions of other worlds in which no life was known to exist. Thus in the vast immensities of astronomical space and geological time life seemed like a tiny glow, a feeble and uncertain flicker, destined one day, when the heat of the sun had cooled to such an extent that the earth was no longer able to support life, to be ignominiously snuffed out in the one corner of the universe which had known it.

Life, then, if the materialists are right, is to be regarded not as the fundamentally significant thing in the universe in terms of which we are to interpret the rest, but as an incidental product thrown up in the haphazard course of evolution, a fortuitous development of matter by means of which matter has become conscious of itself. It is an outside passenger travelling across a fundamentally hostile environment, a passenger, moreover, who will one day finish his journey with as little stir as once in the person of the amoeba he began it. In every direction the material and the brutal underlies and conditions the vital and the spiritual; matter everywhere determines mind, mind nowhere determines matter.

The implications of such a view for the prospects of humanity are not encouraging. Humanity, in fact, is doomed in advance. There was a time when our planet was not suitable for mankind; it was too hot and too moist. A time will come when it will cease to be suitable; it will be too cold and too dry. When the sun goes out, a catastrophe that is bound to be, mankind will long ago have disappeared. The last inhabitants of the earth will be as destitute, as feeble, and as dull-witted as the first. They will have forgotten all the arts and all the sciences. They will huddle wretchedly in caves in the sides of the glaciers that will roll their transparent masses over the half-obliterated ruins of the cities where men now think and love, suffer and hope. The last desperate survivors of mankind will know nothing of our genius, nothing of our civilisation. One day, the last man, callous alike to hate and love, will exhale to the unfriendly sky the last human breath and the globe will go rolling on, bearing with it through the silent fields of space the ashes of humanity, the pictures of Michelangelo, and the remnants of the Greek marbles frozen to its icy surface.

CHAPTER III

MODERN MATERIALISM
PAVLOV AND BEHAVIOURISM

Introductory.

Before I proceed to a criticism of the materialist scheme outlined in the previous chapter, it is necessary to describe the development of materialist views which in recent years has taken place in psychology. This development has been highly successful, with the result that, as I pointed out in the first chapter, the tendency of much contemporary psychology runs in a contrary direction to that of physics and biology. The latter favour a purposive, at times an idealist interpretation of things; they vindicate the independence of mind and even assert its priority over matter; psychology, on the other hand, is inclined to belittle the importance of mind, and to describe the behaviour of the living organism in terms appropriate to a highly complicated automatic machine.

This tendency on the part of modern psychology culminates in the movement known as Behaviourism. Behaviourism is the most widely discussed theory in modern psychology; in America it is on the whole the prevalent view among psychologists—its leading exponent, Dr. Watson, is an American—and even the works of those psychologists who do not accept Behaviourism have consciously or unconsciously been profoundly modified by it. Behaviourism is the logical development of the movement which originated with the psycho-physical parallelism described in the last chapter. Behaviourism does not actually deny the existence of mind, or consciousness; it contents itself with the assertion that, if there is such a thing as consciousness, we cannot know anything about it. But, although we cannot see what a man thinks, we can observe what he does. Hence, our knowledge of other people's psychology is based upon and confined to the observation of their bodily movements. Let us, then, says the Behaviourist, see how far we can go in the attempt to explain people's actions without supposing that they think at all. It is surprising, it is more than surprising, it is humiliating, to find to what lengths an explanation on these lines can be pushed.

The Relevance of Pavlov's work.

Behaviourism has derived its most powerful support from the theory of the conditioned reflex. The theory of the conditioned reflex is associated with the name of the Russian psychologist, Pavlov, whose experiments on dogs may come to be regarded in fifty years' time as constituting a milestone in thought, not less noteworthy than Darwin's *Origin of Species* or the theory of Relativity. Before I endeavour to give some account of Pavlov's experiments, it will be desirable to point out their relevance for the mind-body problem.

One of the great difficulties of the materialist hypothesis outlined in the last chapter is to explain why, if all mental activities are ultimately to be regarded as bodily movements, and all bodily movements are to be interpreted as responses to stimuli, comparatively simple stimuli should be capable of producing such a bewildering variety and complexity of so-called mental effects.

Materialists point to the enormous complexity of the nervous system and the brain, emphasise the fact that our knowledge of the mode of their working is still in its infancy, and express the view that future research will exhibit connections between stimuli and responses which at present seem totally unrelated. But when every allowance is made for these considerations, the theory that we are asked to accept of the ultimate determination of all mental activities by bodily stimuli still stretches most people's powers of credence to the full.

Let us suppose, for example, that I am sitting dozing in an armchair after dinner. My mind wanders, my attention is relaxed. Presently, however, I begin to think about a lecture I am to deliver next week. The occasion is one that I dread, and the ordeal fills me with nervous apprehension; so much so, that I become restless, leave my chair, and begin to pace the room. Here, one would normally say, is an example of spontaneous mental activity, namely expectation tinged with dread, producing certain physiological occurrences. The mind here is cause, and the bodily movements effect. But the normal explanation being ruled out by the materialist theory of causation as proceeding always from the body to the mind, some other must be found.

In some way my apprehension of next week's lecture must be explained in terms of responses to bodily stimuli. What, then, are the stimuli to which my body is exposed? They are roughly of two kinds, external and internal. The external stimuli are constituted by the warmth of the fire upon my face, and the pressure of the sides and seat of the chair against my back and legs. The internal stimuli are constituted by the activity of my bodily organs which accompanies digestion.

The latter are of two kinds, immediate and delayed. The immediate internal stimuli are provided by the actual processes of digestion; the delayed internal stimuli as the result of similar processes stretching back into the remote past. For example, a certain condition of the liver consequent upon eating curries in India for thirty years, may now result in ill temper, indigestion and a tendency to curse the servants. Thus the events in my body which determine present ill temper, are the results of curry stimuli applied in the past whose total effect is only now making itself felt.

Now the assertion that these combined stimuli, external and internal, cause responses in my body of such a kind that what by courtesy I call my mind is induced by them to envisage a lecture which does not yet exist, while not capable of logical disproof, stands in need of considerable justification. And it is precisely this justification that

Pavlov's experiments with conditioned reflexes in dogs purport to provide.

I

PAVLOV'S EXPERIMENTS

These experiments are in essence very simple. Let us suppose that a hungry dog is offered his dinner. When he sees a plate of food, his mouth will water. The mouth watering is a perfectly natural and automatic reaction in which the dog's mind, if any, plays no part. The plate of food is called an unconditioned stimulus; the mouth watering (salivation) an unconditioned response. Screening the dog from all disturbing influences, Pavlov proceeded to sound a buzzer simultaneously with the presentation of the dinner. This was done on a number of occasions. Presently the buzzer was sounded alone, and the dog's mouth watered as before. When the buzzer produced the salivation appropriate to the dinner, the buzzer was known as a conditioned stimulus, and the salivation as a conditioned response. From this simple experiment a number of highly interesting consequences were found to follow.

(i) *Inhibition.* If the buzzer which has been conditioned as a stimulus is sounded several times in rapid succession without the dinner, it fails to produce salivation. The conditioned response is, in other words, inhibited. But the inhibition is temporary only, that is to say, it was found that, if after a lapse of a few days the buzzer was again sounded, the dog salivated as before.

(ii) *Inhibition improved by practice.* If the process described in (i) is repeated several times, the inhibition of the conditioned response to the buzzer is found to occur more rapidly with each repetition. The buzzer has, however, only to be re-accompanied by the food on one occasion to be immediately restored as a conditioned stimulus.

The biological value of this inhibition of responses that

no longer serve a useful purpose is obvious. By virtue of inhibition organisms are enabled to adjust themselves to changing needs and circumstances, instead of wasting time and energy by continuing to respond to stimuli which have ceased to be significant.

(iii) *Discrimination.* Let us suppose that a note of a certain pitch has become conditioned as a stimulus for salivation. At first any neighbouring note produces a conditioned response; but if a number of neighbouring notes are frequently sounded, and the original note alone is followed by food, the conditioned response to the neighbouring notes is inhibited. The dog's organism, in other words, learns by practice to pick out those stimuli which are important and to ignore the rest.

The phenomenon suggests an interesting analogy with the behaviour of human beings. When we learn that a certain stimulus x has a certain significance, but that similar stimuli x_1, x_2 have not, we respond to x but not to x_1 and x_2. We call this behaviour 'grasping the meaning of x'; but, if we take the analogy of the dog seriously, we may infer that it is not necessary to postulate a mind which understands 'the meaning' to explain behaviour such as would normally imply understanding meaning.

(iv) *Combinations.* In a case in which the note of the buzzer had been conditioned as a stimulus, the note of the buzzer plus a flash of white light evoked no response. Again a human analogy suggests itself. A thirsty man responds to a bottle of colourless liquid by raising it to his mouth and drinking. But if he sees the word 'Poison' inscribed on the bottle, the response to the colourless liquid stimulus is inhibited.

(v) *Delayed Conditioned Reflexes.* Let us suppose that a buzzer has been conditioned as a stimulus for salivation. The buzzer is on a number of occasions followed by food at gradually increasing intervals extending in the end to two and a half minutes. In due course the dog's anatomy learns not to salivate when the buzzer is sounded, but to delay salivation until two and a half minutes afterwards.

There is a struggle here between two kinds of impulses, an excitatory and an inhibitory. The excitatory impulse (to salivate) caused by the buzzer is prevented from operating during the prescribed interval by the inhibitory. Responses, which in human beings require careful timing, may be cited as an analogy. One learns at cricket to wait for the ball and not to lash out directly one sees it.

(vi) *Inhibition of inborn reflexes.* Natural unconditioned responses can, it was found, be entirely inhibited. An electric shock, gradually increasing in strength until it would normally be considered intensely painful, could by suitable conditioning be made to evoke mouth watering, tail wagging and other symptoms of pleasure. The cricketer, delighted by catching a hard ball travelling at speed, or the bather entering ice-cold water, here suggest themselves.

(vii) *Disinhibition.* The experiments so far described took place in circumstances in which the dogs were shielded from all disturbing stimuli. When these occurred they were found to extinguish the inhibitions described above, although, provided the disturbance was not too great, the excitatory responses, both unconditioned and conditioned, were not interfered with. This inhibiting of inhibitions by the intrusion of irrelevant stimuli is called 'Disinhibition'. Again we get an illuminating light on human psychology. Effective functioning in life depends, it is obvious, upon an elaborately maintained set of inhibitions. A grown man does not and must not respond to all the stimuli which produce action in children and half-wits. The effect of any extraneous disturbance is to upset this delicate fabric of inhibitions. A man with toothache, a corn, or a nail in his shoe, finds his self-control impaired, and gives way inadvisably and often disastrously to gusts of irritation and fits of temper. The football player who is being 'barracked' fails to time the ball correctly; alcohol again weakens nominal inhibition, so that under its influence we respond to the ever present but normally inhibited impulses to boast and lie.

On the basis of these and similar experiments, of which a few examples have been given, Pavlov has drawn up a rough sketch of the workings of the brain.

Pavlov's account of the brain.

The brain is the receiving station at which a continual stream of impulses is arriving from all parts of the body. These impulses are of two sorts, excitatory and inhibitory, and between them there is constant play and conflict. As we live and learn the first simple plan is scored over by a number of new lines, the conditioned reflexes. The nature of our response to any given stimulus will, in other words, be determined by the conditioning of that stimulus, that is to say, by the nature of the stimuli with which in the past it has been associated. As life proceeds, it is found necessary to inhibit some of our responses both unconditioned and conditioned, and a further picture, this time of inhibitions and discriminations, is scored over the original plan. The whole process, as Pavlov envisages it, is automatic. For the formation of these brain maps we are as little responsible as for the line patterns on the palms of our hands. It follows that the way in which the brain reacts to a stimulus, since it takes place in accordance with the lines of the plan, will be as automatically determined as the salivation of the dog to the conditioned stimulus of the buzzer. When it is remembered that the way in which the brain reacts determines, on this view, the way in which we think, that our thinking, in fact, simply *is* the movements of our brains, the importance of Pavlov's experiments for the materialist hypothesis is obvious.

I cannot here describe in detail the various laws which Pavlov derives from this conception of the ground plan of the brain, laws which are regulative of its workings.[1]

[1] Those who are interested are recommended to read Pavlov's *Lectures on Conditioned Reflexes.*

Two, which embody the opposite tendencies of excitation and inhibition, may be mentioned.

Induction.

The first law, that of Induction, is to the effect that any part of the brain which is affected by an impulse whether of excitation or of inhibition tends to cause the opposite reaction, inhibition when it is excited, excitation when it is inhibited, in the remainder. Thus, when there is concentration, the activity of the rest of the brain tends to be inhibited. When the concentration is habitual and intense, it has a tendency to grow into what is known as an obsession, the obsessed person being literally unable to mobilise his brain except in relation to the matter obsessing him.

Boredom and Sleep.

The second law, which is the opposite of the first, asserts that the excitation or inhibition of any part of the brain tends to spread through the remainder. This is particularly the case in regard to inhibition. If a meaningless stimulus is repeated several times, the natural curiosity response, the 'What's that?' reflex as it is called, is inhibited. This inhibition tends to spread through the brain as a whole. Hence a monotonous noise, the wheels of a train or the lap of water against the sides of a boat, tends to send people to sleep, as the continual inhibition of the natural 'What's that?' reflex spreads through the brain. Inhibition spread is probably the reason why we feel sleepy when bored, the inhibition of the natural response of attention to conversation when the converser is a bore gradually spreading through the brain and making the sufferer sleepy. Sleep is an active, not a passive, process; it is non-localised inhibition, the higher centres of the brain inhibiting the responses of the other centres to the stimuli which normally excite them.

This inhibition of response to a monotonous noise which has become boring can, like any other inhibition, be disinhibited by the process described in (vii) above. Thus a dog who had ceased to pay attention to it when distracted by the stimulus of some further novelty, for example, a flash of light, began again to respond by salivation to the tick of a metronome. Similarly a person sitting alone in a room will normally be unconscious of the tick of a clock, but, if suddenly startled, as for example by a fall of coal from the grate, will begin to notice the clock tick.

Nervous disorders.

Pavlov's work throws an interesting light upon the nature of nervous diseases. His view is that such so-called affections of the mind as hysteria and neurasthenia are the result of a too violent or too prolonged collision between two sets of nervous impulses, excitatory and inhibitory, in the brain. Pavlov has devised experiments for producing clashes of contradictory impulses in his dogs. For example, a circular luminous disc is conditioned as a stimulus for salivation; a flat elliptical shape is not. On a number of succeeding days the dog is presented with ellipses which grow gradually less flat and more circular. The interesting question is, when will he confuse the two shapes, the conditioned circular and the unconditioned elliptical, and what will happen when he does? What in fact happened was that the dog lost his temper. He grew excitable, yelped, forgot all the inhibitions he had so carefully learned, and salivated to even the flattest ellipse. Even outside the experiment room the dog remained bad tempered and irritable, and it was some time before he had sufficiently recovered his normal equanimity to permit of the experiments being resumed.

Here, it is obvious, we have the canine analogy for a nervous breakdown. Nervous breakdowns occur when the machinery of the brain is unable to cope with too violently opposed streams of contradictory impulses. Breakdowns are broadly of two kinds. The first represents the predominance of the excitatory impulses over the inhibitory; all normal inhibitions are temporarily extinguished; any stimulus becomes conditioned for almost any response, with the result that it is impossible to tell what the patient will say or do next. Hysterical disturbances are obviously of this type. In the second class of case the inhibitory impulses blot out the excitatory; carefully established conditioned responses disappear; the patient is languid and bored, and it seems impossible to stimulate his interest. Mental affections of this kind are familiar as neurasthenia.

Excess of inhibitory over excitatory, or of excitatory over inhibitory impulses also throws light on temperamental differences between dogs. It was found that the generality of dogs belonged to one or other of two main types. In dogs belonging to the first, conditioned responses were readily established, but inhibitions only with difficulty. Dogs of this type were excitable, aggressive, lively, curious, apt to lose self-control. Those of the second type were given to excess of inhibition. Conditioned responses established with difficulty were easily extinguished; inhibitions were rapidly set up. These dogs were stolid, sedate, incurious and inclined to be cowardly. Again the analogy with human beings is fairly obvious.

Bearing of Pavlov's Work.

It is time to relate the conclusions of these highly important experiments to the general subject of this chapter, the interpretation of psychology in terms of physiology. The main difficulty which this interpretation has to face is, as I pointed out above, the variety of the responses which may be called out by a simple physical stimulus and the difficulty of establishing their relation to the alleged stimulus. How, it was asked, could a simple stimulus produce such irrelevant, various and apparently disproportionate effects? The importance of Pavlov's work is that it enables us to see how this irrelevance, this variety and this apparent dispro-portionateness of effect can be accounted for. The response to a stimulus is, it appears, determined by the way in which it has been conditioned; hence any stimulus may, within reason, produce almost any response; while the experiment of the ellipse which gradually became more circular shows how the appearance of a luminous disc may lead to a nervous breakdown.

If this is true of dogs, it is markedly more true of human beings. Endowed with vastly more complicated brains, exposed to a much greater variety of stimuli, responding with greater rapidity and sensitiveness, we are far more subject to conditioning than the animals upon which Pavlov experimented. Some, indeed, hold that our characters, our personalities, our motives, our conduct, indeed the whole tenor of our lives, may be explained in terms of the conditioning of our responses.

II

SOME ACCOUNT OF BEHAVIOURISM

(1) *Difficulties of Introspection.*

It is upon this assumption that Behaviourism, the most convincing and coherent attempt to interpret psychology without introducing the conception of mind, is based. As I pointed out above, it is not true that the Behaviourist denies the existence of mind. He contents himself with denying its efficacy. 'If it exists,' he says in effect, 'we can know nothing about it. Therefore I am going to see how far I can go in the direction of interpreting psychology without mentioning it.'

He dispenses, therefore, with the traditional method of psychological investigation, introspection, since intro-spection presumes that there is a mind whose contents it is possible to examine, and resolutely refuses to employ any of the expressions hitherto current in psychology, such as consciousness, instinct, thought, image, sentiment, on the ground that, since these cannot be observed, there is no reason to suppose that they are separately existent factors in our make-up. If it be objected that I can by introspection acquaint myself with my own images, the Behaviourist answers, either that I am inventing the images which I expected to find or that, if I really do find them, I have put them there by my act of looking for them. Whether we accept the Behaviourist account of the matter or not, we must admit that the study of mind as traditionally conducted labours under one very grave disability. In psychology the mind which is investigated is the same as the mind by which the process of investigation is being conducted. Hence, it is said, it is insensibly and inevitably affected by the fact that it is being investigated. While the atom may be supposed to be unaffected by the fact that the physicist is examining it,[1] the mind which is being looked into is necessarily different from the mind that is not, being affected by its own act of self-examination. Moreover, while there seems to be a public world of physics which is the same for all observers,[2] the mind is private to each observer, and a man's report of what he finds there cannot be checked or verified by reference to any external standard. It is for these reasons, the Behaviourist complains, that psychology, as it has been studied in the past, is fundamentally unscientific. Repeated experiments under controlled conditions the results of which can be checked and verified are of the essence of scientific method; but, where the object is private to the experimenter, there can be neither control nor verification, and the fact that it is different on each occasion on which it is examined precludes the possibility of repetition.

(ii) *Meaning of 'Behaviour'*.

These are only some of the reasons which lead the Behaviourist to dispense with the concept of mind. They

[1-2] For recent doubts on these points, see the next chapter, pp. 66, 91–93.

constitute what might be called the negative case for
Behaviourism. On the positive side the Behaviourist
confines himself and, if the considerations adduced
above are valid, rightly confines himself to the study of
what can be observed by himself and others. What can
be observed is what people do, that is to say, the way in
which they behave. The word 'behaviour' is used to
mean anything that the body does, whether external
and therefore visible, as when at sight of a ghost the
hair stands on end, or internal and unseen as when
under the influence of the same stimulus the adrenal
gland secretes fluid. Hence the kind of question which
the Behaviourist asks is, 'Given an object or situation,
what will the individual do when confronted with it?' or
vice versa, 'When an individual behaves in a certain
manner, what is the object or situation which caused
him so to behave?'

It is clear that, if the concept of mind is to be excluded
from the interpretation of psychology, a living organism
must in the last resort be presumed to be of the same
character as an automatic machine. It will, that is to
say, only 'behave' in so far as it is caused to do so by a
specific stimulus; and this stimulus must be a physical
stimulus. It is the object of the Behaviourist, therefore,
to describe all behaviour in terms of responses to stimuli.
The word stimulus is used in the widest connotation to
denote any change in the environment or the physical
conditions of the organism. To prevent a bird from
building a nest or an animal from feeding or mating, is
to expose it to a stimulus in the shape of a change in its
physical conditions. Similarly the word response is used
in a wide sense to cover any form of behaviour from
going to sleep to addressing meetings, and from having
babies to writing books. The main purpose of psychology
is to be able to assign the cause for a particular kind
of behaviour, by specifying the stimulus which produced
it; to say, in other words, 'A does x because of y'. In so
far as psychology is able to do this, it becomes scientific.

In establishing connections between stimulus and response the Behaviourist makes wide use of the conception of the conditioned reflex.

(iii) *Conditioning the responses of children.*

The child comes into the world equipped with a number of very simple responses. These responses are of the nature of automatic reflex actions. A reflex action is one in the causation of which neither brain nor mind plays any necessary part. A simple type of reflex is the jerking forward of the crossed leg when the skin is struck by the side of the hand just below the knee. Hence, to say that the new-born baby exhibits a number of unconditioned responses by which its behaviour is determined, is equivalent to saying that it is an automatic mechanism.

As a result of numerous experiments on young babies, Dr. Watson estimates that there are in the normal human child only three types of unconditioned responses which can subsequently be conditioned. There is the love response produced by tickling or stroking, the fear response produced by a sudden loud noise or the feeling of being left without support, and the rage response evoked by a hampering of the child's bodily movements.[1] Other responses are rapidly built up by conditioning, while the unconditioned responses come to be evoked by new and therefore conditioned stimuli. Thus the mother's face produces a smile, because it has become a conditioned stimulus for the love response through being associated with gentle stroking.

Now all this has an important practical bearing. It is obvious that, if the Behaviourist view is true in all that it asserts, and if also we could obtain sufficient knowledge of the process of conditioning, we could mould the character of human beings at will. For example, nothing,

---

[1] Sneezing, hiccuping, blinking and what is known as the Babinski reflex, are cited by Dr. Watson as unconditioned reflexes which are not the sources of conditioned reflexes. Yawning and stretching are apparently conditioned.

in Dr. Watson's view, is by nature terrifying to the human being except sudden loud noises and the feeling of being left without support. To prescribe what a baby shall fear throughout its life, it is only necessary to associate the object, or person whom it is desired that it should fear with the noise stimulus or the lack of support stimulus.

More important in practice is the extinguishing of a fear response, which is undesirable. This is effected by unconditioning a conditioned fear response.

Dr. Watson cites experiments conducted with the object of curing a child who was afraid (the fear being, of course, conditioned) of a bowl of goldfish. All the traditional methods of removing fear, bribery, explanation, exhortation, objurgation, appeal to sense of shame, example of other children, had been tried and failed. Dr. Watson's method was to associate the bowl of goldfish with another stimulus, that of the child's dinner. At first the bowl was put at the far end of the table only just within the child's line of vision. Each day at dinner time it was brought a little nearer; finally it was put on the tray with the plate of food without causing fear. The cure was, moreover, permanent, since, according to the explanation which Dr. Watson gives, a definite change had been produced by the unconditioning process in the structures of the child's body.

Aldous Huxley's novel *Brave New World* presents a vivid picture of a society trained and educated on strict Watsonian principles.

(iv) *Behaviourist account of Thinking.*

There is no aspect of human psychology to which Behaviourism is not applied. Even that form of activity which would seem most unamenable to the Behaviourist mode of treatment, the activity of thinking, is included within its scope. Thinking for the Behaviourist is simply talking—talking, that is to say, under one's breath. When one thinks, certain muscles in the larynx are said to be in

movement and subconsciously to form the words by
means of which one's thought, if one were to speak it,
would be expressed. This movement of the muscles in
the larynx together with other incipient movements in
the hands, in the viscera and indeed all over the body,
is held by the Behaviourist to accompany the act of
thinking. More accurately, they constitute it; for thinking, on the Behaviourist view, simply *is* the occurrence
of those bodily activities which would normally be said
to accompany it.

Thinking, therefore, may be regarded like all other
psychological occurrences, in the light of a response to a
stimulus. Look, says Dr. Watson, at a child playing
with its toys on the nursery floor. You will find that he
talks to them, to them and to himself. If he sees you,
he will as likely as not stop talking openly and begin
mumbling to himself, not wishing you to hear him.
Sooner or later his mumbling will probably be stopped
by grown-ups, and he will subside into silence. But this
silence does not mean that he is not still talking. He is,
but he is now doing it silently. This silent talking is what
we call thinking. The great advantage of thinking as a
mode of behaviour over talking is that there are no
external signs of thinking in our *observable* behaviour.
Thinking, in fact, cannot be observed; therefore, we can
think what we please when we please. But the circumstance that we do it unobserved should not blind us to
the fact that thinking is still essentially a bodily response
to the stimulus of a certain situation, its development
being derivable by logical steps from the muttering of
the child to his toys.

(v) *Word Conditioning*.

Because of the other bodily movements which accompany, or rather which *are* thinking, thinking does not
always or necessarily consist of words. Animals, for
example, think without words. In ourselves, however,
verbal thinking is usually dominant. The great advan-

tage of verbal thinking is that it enables us to deal with objects in their absence, the word for the object coming by association to stand for and to take the place of the object. This substitution of word for object is an example of conditioning. Indeed the whole use of language to convey meanings relating to things and persons not visibly present depends upon the establishment of conditioned responses. If we see a burglar in the room, we take our revolver from under the pillow, call for the police, or hand over our loose cash, according to temperament. If we are *told* that a burglar is in the next room, although there is as yet no visible stimulus, we may nevertheless react in the same way. The word 'burglar' in fact first causes us to make the same responses as the object 'burglar'. A child learns to understand words as he learns any other form of conditioned reflex. If you say bottle whenever you give the child his bottle, he presently begins to react to the word bottle as he does to the object bottle; that is to say, his mouth waters. When he responds in this way, we say that he understands the word bottle.

When we react in the same way to a word as we would react to that for which the word stands, we are said to know the meaning of the word. Thus, according to the Behaviourist theory, a person may be said to know the meaning of the word *x*, if the associative effects of *x*, when he hears it, are similar to those of the thing which the word *x* is used to describe.

Comment and Criticism.

To examine further this highly intriguing theory of psychology would take me beyond the scope of this book. I accordingly conclude this chapter with two brief comments; the object of the first is to establish the relevance of Behaviourism to my main theme; of the second, to suggest a doubt as to its validity.

(1) I noted in the Introductory Chapter as one of the most puzzling features of modern thought the contradictory answers which it suggests to the traditional

questions of philosophy. Physics is idealist in tendency; biology points to a purposive theory of evolution; but psychology, I pointed out, has on the whole remained mechanistic and deterministic. In so describing the tendencies of psychology, I had in mind chiefly Behaviourism, Behaviourism and the implications of psycho-analysis, to which I have devoted a later chapter. Behaviourism exemplifies the generalisation in two ways:

(a) It denies that there is any non-material element in our make-up, mind, soul, spirit, call it what you will, which influences our behaviour. So far as psychology is concerned, we can, it holds, get along very well on the assumption that the human being is all body. As for consciousness, it is a by-product of bodily processes which sometimes but quite incidentally accompanies them. It does not cause the processes it accompanies, and it is not necessary that we should be conscious of them in order that they may occur.

(b) If the individual is all body, or can at least be satisfactorily explained on this assumption, his behaviour will ultimately be explicable in terms of the same laws as those which determine the motions of other bodies. These laws are in the first instance those of dynamics and mechanics, more ultimately those of chemistry and physics.

In so far as the motions of matter are determined—and the Behaviourist believes that they are—the activity of living organisms must be determined too. Therefore, if Behaviourism is right, we are merely complicated automata.

Conclusion (a) favours materialism; conclusion (b) mechanism. Summing up we may say that on this view, whatever may be the function of mind or spirit in the universe, it plays no part in the interpretation of the psychology of living human beings.

(2) But in establishing this conclusion Behaviourism runs a considerable risk of destroying the foundation on

which it is based. It is not my intention in this book to criticise the various theories which I shall endeavour to expound; but it is pertinent to point out that, if all thought is accurately and exhaustively described as a set of responses to stimuli, responses which may be analysed into movements of the larynx and the brain, then this applies also to the thought which constitutes the Behaviourist view of psychology.

If Behaviourism is correct in what it asserts, the doctrine of Behaviourism reflects nothing but a particular condition of the bodies of Behaviourists. Similarly, rival theories of psychology merely reflect the conditions prevailing in the bodies of rival psychologists. To ask which of the different theories is true is as meaningless as to ask which of the various blood pressures of the theorists concerned is true, since the chains of reasoning which constitute their theories, like their blood pressures, are merely bodily functions, bearing relation not to the outside facts which they purport to describe, but to the bodily conditions of which they are a function.

This kind of criticism is valid against any theory which seeks to impugn the validity of reason by representing it either as a function of the body or as the tool of an unconscious and non-rational self. In this latter connection we shall find grounds for restating it in a later chapter.

CHAPTER IV

THE WORLD OF MODERN PHYSICS

I

INTRODUCTORY

Physics and Psychology.

I described in the last chapter the success which has attended the efforts of modern psychologists to interpret the behaviour of a living organism on the assumption that it is all body and that it works like a machine. This success is very far from being absolute; nevertheless, it is considerable. Behaviourism has managed to push its explanations considerably further than its opponents expected, while the mechanist interpretation of psychology has received a considerable stimulus from Pavlov's work. It is an ironical commentary upon this success that at the moment when it is apparently most pronounced it should be robbed of most of its significance by recent developments in physics.

The concepts in terms of which Behaviourist psychologists have sought to explain the workings of mind, the concepts of mechanism, causation, motion, energy, matter, are taken from physics; yet the moment when they are being applied with the greatest confidence to psychology is also the moment when they are being abandoned or declared to be meaningless by the physicist.

Materialistically disposed psychologists have tried to show that the human being is all matter and that it is unnecessary to introduce the conception of mind as an explanatory principle, under the influence of the assumptions that matter is simple and that physics knows what it is and how it behaves. But the explanation of the apparent complexity of a human being in terms of his nerves, glands and brain, is robbed of most of its value when we discover that it is impossible to say what is meant by nerves, glands and brain. To interpret the workings of mind in terms of changes in the body is, indeed, a negligible gain if we do not know what the nature of a bodily change is.

Psychologists again have displayed ingenuity in exhibiting free will as an illusion and showing that the human being works like a machine. The attempt was worth making so long as we really knew, or thought we did, how a machine worked. The nineteenth-century physicist, as we have seen, envisaged the world as a vast machine. Hence, it seemed reasonable to suppose that the laws of physics would ultimately be found to apply to the individual contents of the world including living organisms. But this view of the physical world is no longer held, with the result that, as Professor Eddington puts it, 'Physics to-day is not likely to be attracted by a type of explanation of the mind which it would scornfully reject for its own aether.'[1]

Again, Dr. Watson, as we have seen, holds that observation of bodily behaviour is the only legitimate method for psychology. What people think is, he points out, private and cannot be observed; what they do is public and can. Hence, he exhorts us to study behaviour and not to make unjustifiable inferences about the *mind* of the behaver. That we can observe other people's behaviour he accepts unquestioningly as his premise; it never seems to occur to him that it may be a highly questionable assumption. Yet this, if certain theories of perception founded on physics are to be believed, is precisely what it is. 'When Dr. Watson watches rats in mazes, what he knows, apart from difficult inferences, are certain events in himself';[2] so Earl Russell, who holds that modern physics requires the view that the only events we can directly know are those which happen in our own bodies. Thus, at the very moment

[1] Eddington. *Science and the Unseen World*, p. 21.
[2] Russell. *An Outline of Philosophy*, p. 140.

when the materialist psychology appears to be pushing its claim in its own sphere with the greatest success, the ground is being cut from under its feet by physics. The developments in physics which have produced this somewhat paradoxical position I shall try to describe in the present chapter.

II

THE INSIGNIFICANCE OF LIFE

Modern physicists take a very different view of the nature of the material world from that which I briefly sketched in the second chapter. The old conception of matter as a simple obvious thing lying out there in space has been replaced by something infinitely more mysterious and elusive; much too mysterious and much too elusive to form an adequate foundation for a materialist theory of the universe. The nineteenth-century scientists, impressed by the discoveries of geology and astronomy, laid stress upon the insignificance of life and mind in an apparently mindless universe. If by life is meant human life, if by mind, man's mind, the twentieth century has seen little reason to alter the estimate of the nineteenth. Subsequent discovery has, indeed, endorsed it. As facts have accumulated, the rarity of life in space, its brevity in time have been ever more conclusively demonstrated. Sir James Jeans has presented the upshot of these facts in a sufficiently picturesque way.

(i) *Facts of Astronomy.*

There are, first, facts relating to the insignificance of man's planet. There is not, as astronomers used until recently to think, one system of stars but many. Each of these systems came into being as the result of the gradual break-up of a spiral nebula, to which Sir James Jeans gives the name of 'an island universe'.

About two million such nebulae are visible through the great 100-inch telescope on Mount Wilson, and Sir

James Jeans quotes an estimate to the effect that the whole universe is about a thousand million times as big as the area of space visible through this telescope. Each spiral nebula contains enough matter to make a thousand million of our sun. If a thousand million is multiplied by two million and that again by a thousand million (the average number of the estimated stars in each nebula), the resultant figure gives some indication of the probable number of stars in the universe. It is, Sir James Jeans estimates, 'probably something like the total number of grains of sand on all the sea-shores of the world'.[1] Now the sun is one such grain of sand; yet the sun is a million times as big as the earth and 300,000 times as massive!

In spite of this immense number of stars space is almost empty. 'If we place an apple at the centre of the earth and place a grape fruit, two more apples, two apricots and a currant in the six continents of the earth's surface, we shall have a fairly good scale-model of the arrangement in space of our sun and its six nearest neighbours'.[2] There is no reason to suppose that space as a whole is more densely crowded than the region adjacent to our sun; there is, indeed, some reason to suppose that large areas of space are less crowded. With regard to the size of space as a whole, we are told that light which takes a seventh of a second to travel round the earth takes 'probably something like 100,000 million years to travel round the universe'.[3]

(ii) *Rarity of Planetary Systems.*

Secondly, there are facts showing the fortuitous character of life, and the rarity in the universe of the conditions in which alone we can suppose it to be possible. Life, as we know it, can occur only on those tiny specks

[1] Sir James Jeans. *The Mysterious Universe*, p. 1.
[2] Sir James Jeans. 'The Birth of the World', Harmsworth's *Universal History*, Part I, p. 66.
[3] Sir James Jeans. 'Eos', p. 18.

of burnt-out ash which are planets. According to the tidal theory of the formation of planets, a necessary condition of the occurrence of a planetary system is the close approach of two stars in a certain condition of development. The odds against such an approach are very great. 'Exact calculation demonstrates that, with the stars moving as they now are in the neighbourhood of the sun, in a period of seven million million years only about one star in a hundred thousand will approach near enough to another for the birth of a solar system to be possible, and even then there are odds of perhaps ten to one against a solar system actually being formed.'[1] Thus the occurrence of a planetary system is an exceedingly rare accident, and the number of planets in the universe on which conditions even remotely approximating to those in which life, as we know it, alone is possible, is exceedingly small. We should have to visit thousands of millions of stars before finding a planetary system as recent as our own. Elsewhere, Sir James Jeans estimates that the zones of the universe in which life, as we know it, is possible added together constitute less than a thousand million-millionth part of the whole of space.[2]

(iii) *Brevity of Life*.

A third set of facts which point in the same direction are time facts. The life of our own planetary system, judged in relation to an astronomical time scale, is very short; the period of life upon the earth, judged in relation to a geological time scale, is very short, and the period of human life, judged in relation to a biological time scale, is very short. To take the biological time scale alone, it is estimated that the past of life upon the earth, from its earliest appearance in the shape of specks of protoplasm floating in the tidal scum of the shores of the earth's first seas, is roughly about twelve hundred

[1] Sir James Jeans. 'The Birth of the World', Harmsworth's *Universal History*, Part I, p. 72.
[2] Sir James Jeans. *The Mysterious Universe*, p. 5.

million years.[1] The past of human life from Neanderthal man up to the present day is about one million years; of civilised human life, admitting as civilisation all doubtful cases, about four thousand.

The cumulative effect of facts of this kind is to suggest that the occurrence of life is an unplanned accident in a fundamentally lifeless universe. Taking the facts accumulated by science at their face value, the only possible conclusion, in Sir James Jeans's view, is that 'one tiny corner at least, and possibly several tiny corners, of this universe of atoms has chanced to become conscious for a time, but was designed in the end, still under the action of blind mechanical forces, to be frozen out and again leave a lifeless world'.[2]

It cannot, then, be suggested that, taking the facts at their face value, physicists to-day are inclined to attribute an importance which the nineteenth-century world would have refused either to life in general or to human life in particular.

But the question arises, how far are we justified in taking the facts collected by the physical sciences at their face value? Is it really the case that this material universe that the sciences study, and about which they collect such staggering statistics, is the only universe that there is? Is it, indeed, even quite what it seems? Modern physicists are inclined to answer emphatically that it is not, and it is to the reasons for this answer that we must now turn our attention. Out of a number of different lines of argument, all of which tend to the same conclusion, that the physical world is neither all that there is nor such as at first sight we believe it to be, I will select three as fairly representative of current trends of thought in physics. I do not wish to suggest that all physicists would subscribe to them, but each is advanced and sponsored by one or more physicists of eminence and authority.

[1] The estimate is very rough; it may be incorrect by hundreds of million years.

[2] Sir James Jeans. *The Mysterious Universe*, p. 148.

c

III

A. PHYSICS AS THE SCIENCE OF ABSTRACTION

It cannot have escaped the notice of anybody who has the most cursory acquaintance with scientific thought that the world of physics is very different from the world of everyday life. The latter is qualitatively rich and varied, the former qualitatively simple; the latter contains many features, smells, for example, tastes and colours, which are not to be found in the former. Indeed, apart from motion, shape and number, it is difficult to say what characteristics the physicist's world does possess. What account, then, does the physicist give of the qualities which, present in the familiar world, are absent from his own?

I will give a few examples of the way in which he treats them.

The Physicist's treatment of Sense Qualities.

Let us begin with heat. Heat, according to the physicist's account, is caused by or *is* the energy both kinetic and potential of the motion of molecules. Consider, for example, the case of a gas. It consists of molecules of about a hundred-millionth of an inch across with comparatively large spaces between them moving about in all directions with an average speed measured in hundreds of yards a second. The molecules meet and collide and in consequence of their collision the gas has a certain temperature. If the gas is placed in a flame or hot body, the molecules of which it is composed will gain in energy, moving rapidly and colliding more violently. Imperceptibly the temperature of the gas will go up; heat, as we say, is generated. But the cause of this heat is the greater energy of motion of the molecules; or, to put it as a textbook on physics would put it, heat *is* nothing but the energy of motion of molecules.

Similarly sound is said to be caused by, or alternatively to *be*, waves in the atmosphere. These waves vary in length, in frequency of vibration and in mode of vibration. Variations in length determine the loudness, in frequency of vibration the pitch and in mode of vibration the quality of the sound. By the quality of sound I mean that property which distinguishes the note of a trumpet from that, say, of a violin: if the vibrating body, which is the sounding body, moves with a uniform speed from the position of rest to its two extreme positions, the note sounded is of a different quality from that which is produced by a body moving as a pendulum moves—that is, which moves more slowly as it reaches the two extreme positions. Sound, then, is produced by atmospheric waves. Atmospheric waves are described as regions of pressure and rarefication in the atmosphere moving forward with a certain velocity, and the movement of such a region of the atmosphere is the cause of, or simply *is*, sound. Thus the properties of the atmospheric waves which the sounding body gives out determine the character of the sounds which are heard.

Solidity, again, *is*, or is caused by, or is a characteristic of, a certain spatial relationship between atoms. A solid is composed of atoms which are so crowded together that their electrical forces interfere with one another, a liquid of atoms less tightly packed, a gas of atoms still less crowded; in a gas there is enough space between the atoms to enable them to radiate frequencies which can be detected and assessed without entanglement with those given off by neighbouring atoms.

Hardness is caused by the repulsion of electrical forces between the parts of the body by means of which the hardness is felt and the object felt to be hard. If a finger-tip is pressed against a 'hard' table, the electrons and protons composing the finger-tip and those composing the table do not actually make contact, but an electrical repulsion is developed between them. A soft object, a gas, for example, or a liquid, is one in which, the atoms not being closely packed, there is room for the repelled electrons and protons to get away. In a solid, however, this is not the case. The sensation of hardness when we press a solid is caused by the fact that the repelled electrons and protons are unable to move away and are jammed by other electrons and protons close behind them. The greater the pressure, the more the finger-tip is repelled and the greater seems the 'hardness' of the table.

Smell is, or is caused by, or consists of, molecules given off in the form of vapour by the substance which in ordinary language is said to smell. Smell, it is interesting to note, is not even for common sense a property which is attached to the object; a smell, it is thought, is something *given off by* rather than something which *belongs to*.

Most significant of all is the case of colour. Colour is often described as a quality of light; it is, at any rate, intimately bound up with light, so that where there is no light, there is no colour.

Light is, or is caused by, a certain set of wave-lengths of varying frequencies in the electro-magnetic spectrum. Within this section of wave-lengths which are, or which produce, light, certain subsections are earmarked for the different colours. At one end of the section, that containing waves of shortest wave-length and highest frequency, are violet rays; at the other, red rays. Beyond violet are the ultra-violet rays, which are called violet only by courtesy, since they cannot be seen: below red, at the other end of the section, are the infra-red, which equally are red by courtesy only. Between lie the other colours. Thus, just as light waves constitute a particular section of the waves graded according to length and frequency in the electro-magnetic spectrum, most of which are not visible, so each colour is constituted by a subsection of waves of particular frequency and wavelength falling within the light section.

These scientific descriptions of the qualities which

characterise the world of our everyday experience have an important point in common; the scientific objects in terms of which the qualities are analysed are themselves devoid of the qualities in question.

Thus, physics takes the ordinary qualities of the world we perceive and analyses them into something else. The world we see is coloured, the world we hear noisy; but the world of physics is neither coloured nor noisy. What, then, has become of colour and noise? Roughly there are two main answers to this question, the first, that colour and noise are supplied by the mind, or, on some views, by the brain, of the perceiver; the other, that they really are out there in the world, but that physics is incapable of giving any account of them. It can describe the conditions under which they appear and the constituents of which they are composed, but they themselves elude it. Physics on this view is like a cookery book which gives admirable descriptions of currants, flour, eggs and milk, but omits any mention of puddings and cakes. Both these answers are commonly suggested in contemporary thought and both must be examined. I will begin with the first.

How physics abstracts.

Prominent in the writings of many physicists is the view that physical science deals not with things in their completeness as wholes but with certain abstracted aspects of them. These aspects are those which are susceptible of quantitative measurement, speed of motion, for example, or number, or weight. When we say that A is lighter or heavier than B we are making a statement about a quantitative and, therefore, measurable aspect of A. Similarly with temporal and spatial qualities. But consider such a quality as ugliness or wetness. It is absurd to say that one piece of water is twice as wet as another, or that the wetness of cream is more or less wet than the wetness of milk. Wetness, then, is not a quality which can be quantitatively measured, and physics is, therefore, it is said, incapable of dealing with it. All that physics can tell you about wetness is that wetness is a quality of water, and that water is H_2O, that is to say, it is made up of two parts of hydrogen and one of oxygen. But neither hydrogen nor oxygen is wet. What, then, the physicist has done is to substitute for a quality of the familiar world which he cannot measure, wetness, certain quantities, those, namely, of hydrogen and oxygen, that he can. In other words he takes water, abstracts its quantitatively measurable aspects, reaches results about these aspects and ignores the rest.

And classifies.

Again, the method of physics is classification. It classifies things according to their common aspects. Hence, the aspects of a thing with which physics deals must be those which it shares with a number of different things. They must, that is to say, be its common qualities or aspects. It follows that those particular characteristics in respect of which a thing is different from all other things slip through the meshes of scientific analysis. The following example by a recent writer on the methods of science, Mr. Joseph Needham, admirably illustrates the point:

'If the scientific mind is faced with five hundred balls of all shades of grey from pure black to pure white, it will separate them into groups of greys, but these are discontinuous, whereas from the common-sense point of view one could not have less than five hundred groups for all the balls are by definition different. It is only by what has been called an "arbitrary falsification of the object's nature" that classification can be carried out at all. Even in the case of the two black balls, the scientific mind will sweep them into the same box, unconscious of the fact that one of them is slightly less of a sphere than the other, if it happens at the moment to be interested in blackness and not globularity.'[1]

[1] Needham. *The Sceptical Biologist*, p. 248.

Now, there is an important sense in which everything is different from everything else, a sense in which everything is just what it is and nothing else, and being so, is therefore unique. This essential uniqueness of things, which we call their individuality, is accordingly another characteristic of them with which physics on this view is unable to deal. Putting the point generally we may say that science ignores differences and concentrates on likenesses. The scientific investigator says, in effect, 'Let us suppose that we shall get on best by paying no attention to certain aspects of a certain object, and by concentrating our attention on one aspect only. We shall then be able to class it with other objects which have this aspect, and so we shall form a group.'

In other words, 'Let us suppose that we shall get on best by treating things which are really different, as if in certain respects they were alike.'

The conclusion is similar to that already reached; just as science is unable to give an account of the non-quantitative aspects of things, their wetness, for example, or their beauty, so it is unable to give an account of their individuality. And, just as science abstracts for treatment quantitative aspects which can be measured, so also does it abstract common aspects which can be classified. Two points emerge; first, the conclusions of physics are not about real things but about abstracted aspects of them. Secondly, the selection of these abstracted aspects is determined, in part at least, by the mind of the physicist who has abstracted them; there is no necessary reason why anything exactly corresponding to these abstracted aspects should exist outside the physicist's mind. The two points are different although often confused, and I will treat them separately.

Closed Circle of Physics.

The first point is exemplified by an illustration given by Professor Eddington. He instances the case of an elephant sliding down a grassy hillside and considers the account which the ordinary physicist would give of this phenomenon. The physicist wishes, we will suppose, to know how long it will take the elephant to get to the bottom. For the elephant he proceeds to read a weight of two tons, for the sloping hillside an angle of sixty degrees, for the soft, yielding turf a coefficient of friction. Replacing the natural objects given in the question, the elephant, the hillside and the turf, with these pointer readings, namely, two tons, sixty degrees and a co-efficient of friction, he makes certain calculations and produces an answer in terms of seconds, that is to say, in terms of another pointer reading measured on the dial of his watch. But the answer, it is clear, is not an answer which tells us anything about the elephant or about the hillside, the objects with which the problem started, but merely about the relation between certain abstracted features of the elephant and the hillside, those features, namely, which are susceptible of exact quantitative measurement. In so far, then, as the elephant, the hillside and the rest are *real* things which are more than the sum of their weights and angles, in so far as the elephant has, for example, memories and the hillside beauty, science is unable to tell us anything about them.

Physics, then, on Professor Eddington's view, deals with a closed world, the boundaries of which are those quantitative and measurable aspects of things which the physicist has selected as being alone amenable to treatment by his methods.

World of Physics as Symbolic, not Real.

But this is not the whole story, for—and here we come to a further point—the abstracted aspects with which physics deals are not necessarily *out there* in the world at all. They may not be, and Professor Eddington suggests that they in fact are not, objectively real things, which are constituents of the world in their own right, but symbols of real things, symbols which the mind of the scientist has constructed and which reflect the interests and peculiarities of his mind as their maker. These symbols do not at any point bring us into touch with, because they do not form part of, reality; they have meaning only in terms of each other. Hence, the world of physics is a closed circle the circumference of which is constituted by symbols of the physicist's own manufacture. The point will be better understood by means of an example, which I will again take from Professor Eddington. The example, unfortunately, involves the use of technical terms, which I promised in the first chapter scrupulously to avoid. But the promise is broken in the letter rather than in the spirit, since it is not necessary to know what any of the technical terms mean in order to appreciate the force of the example. Not being a mathematical physicist I have not the faintest idea what most of them mean myself. The example relates to the general theory of relativity which, says Professor Eddington, in its analytical form is a statement to the effect that in empty space *potentials* obey certain differential equations. What are potentials? Quantities derived from certain more fundamental quantities called intervals in space-time. What are intervals in space-time? Relations between events measured by scales or clocks. What are scales or clocks? They are pieces of matter. What is matter? There are two answers to this question; I will give the first, the scientist's answer, and reserve the second. 'Confining ourselves to mechanics, which is the subject in which the law of gravitation arises, matter,' says Professor Eddington, 'may be defined as the embodiment of three related physical quantities, mass, momentum and stress.'[1] What are mass, momentum and stress? They are expressions containing *potentials* and their derivatives. But in introducing potentials we have returned to our starting point. All other physical definitions are, according to Professor Eddington, characterised by the same kind of interlocking. 'Electrical force is defined as something which causes motion of

[1] Eddington. *The Nature of the Physical World*, p. 262.

electric charge; an electric charge is something which exerts electric force.'[1]

The structure of modern physics is thus like the structure of the House that Jack built; its various parts are defined purely in terms of each other. They are not realities but, to repeat the expression of which Professor Eddington so frequently makes use, symbols.

And if we ask the question, 'after what model then are we to envisage the external world?' Professor Eddington replies that to answer that question is not the physicist's business. His results do not apply to reality, but only to the aspects of it which his mind has selected for treatment. As to the nature of the something which underlies the symbols, that which the symbols symbolise, the physicist does not know nor, apparently, in his capacity as physicist, care. 'And if to-day you ask a physicist what he has finally made out the aether or the electron to be, the answer will not be a description in terms of billiard balls or fly wheels, or anything concrete; he will point instead to a number of symbols and a set of mathematical equations which they satisfy. What do the symbols stand for? The mysterious reply is given that physics is indifferent to that; it has no means of probing beneath the symbolism.'[2]

Idealist Implications.

But although Professor Eddington in his capacity of physicist can tell us nothing of the reality behind the symbols, there are, he thinks, good grounds for surmising its nature to be mental or spiritual. To indicate what these grounds are it will be necessary to return to the second answer to the question 'What is matter', the one which, I said, I would reserve. The second answer, the answer, at least, that Professor Eddington gives, is that 'Matter is what Mr. X knows'. Matter, in other words, is something which is known by a mind. But,

[1] Eddington. *The Nature of the Physical World*, p. 264.
[2] Eddington. *Science and the Unseen World*, p. 20.

once we have defined matter in terms of mind's knowledge of it, as being that which mind knows, it is found
difficult to resist the further conclusion that matter exists
only in so far as mind knows it, and we are within
measurable distance of an idealist view of the universe,
which insists that mind is primary and matter merely an
aspect or a projection of mind's activity.

This step is in fact taken by Professor Eddington and
its consequences will be briefly considered in the last
section of this chapter. For the present it is sufficient to
emphasise the view of science as dealing not with reality
but with abstracted aspects of it, these being symbols of
the reality behind, of which science itself has no knowledge and can have none.

Nor, although I have chiefly followed Professor Eddington in my exposition of this view, should it be supposed that it is only to be found in his writings. He has,
it is true, been chiefly responsible for its popularisation,
but the view itself in one form or another is coming to be
fairly widely held by a certain school of physicists. Sir
James Jeans, for example, insists no less strongly than
Professor Eddington on the fact that physics does not
give us information about the real nature of material
things, but only about abstractions. The ether is an
abstraction, the ether waves are abstractions, and the
waves which 'make up' an electron exemplify this
'quality of abstractness . . . in a more acute form'. As
for the electron 'isolated in space', it 'provides a perfectly
eventless universe', while the seven-dimensional space
in which wave-mechanics pictures the meeting of two
electrons is described as being, in the view of most
physicists, 'purely fictitious'.[1] The arguments which Sir
James Jeans advances in favour of these conclusions are
similar to those which I have already sketched.

In illustration of the general procedure and limitations of physics Sir James Jeans invokes the famous
simile in the seventh book of Plato's *Republic*. A row of

[1] Sir James Jeans. *The Mysterious Universe*, pp. 120, 121.

prisoners is sitting in a cave, chained so that they can look only in one direction. Behind them a fire is burning, and between the fire and the prisoners is a raised platform along which passes a constant procession of moving things. The prisoners see not the things but the shadows of them cast by the fire upon the wall in front of them; since, however, they can never turn their heads, they do not know this. Sir James Jeans likens the physicist's knowledge of the external world to that of the prisoners; it is a knowledge of shadows. As Sir James Jeans puts it, we live in a world of shadows; science is no more able than is daily experience to introduce us to the originals. It only studies the shadows with greater exactitude. Of the reality behind the shadows science can give us no knowledge.

IV

B. THE INDIRECTNESS OF OUR KNOWLEDGE
OF MATTER

The modern picture of the atom.

It is now fairly generally known that the nineteenth-century conception of the atom as a little, hard, solid ball of homogeneous stuff has been abandoned. It has been replaced,[1] or until the last few years it had been replaced, by the more complex conception of the atom as a miniature solar system. In the centre there is a number of packets of positive electricity known as protons, which constitute the nucleus; around the nucleus there rotate at various distances and in irregular orbits, smaller packets of negative electricity, the electrons. The charge of positive electricity in each proton is exactly equal to the negative charge of each rotating electron. The number of protons forming the nucleus is, however,

[1] There have been more recent developments still which do not lend themselves to description in non-technical language. Moreover, the concept of the atom to which these later developments point outruns the capacities of the pictorial imagination.

considerably larger normally than that of the rotating electrons, the balance being redressed by the presence of further negative electrons embedded in the nucleus.

Thus in the helium atom the nucleus has a positive charge of four (four protons of positive electricity); with it are associated two electrons of negative electricity, while two more planetary electrons circulate round the nucleus. The simplest atom, the hydrogen atom, consists of one proton of positive electricity, and one electron of exactly equal charge going round it; the most complicated, the unanium atom, has 238 protons and 146 electrons in the nucleus, and 92 planetary electrons outside the nucleus.

There were from the first several peculiar features in this conception of the atom. For example, the electrons which one would have expected to find rotating round the nucleus in any orbit, were discovered in practice to restrict themselves to a very small number of the orbits that were possible, and always to travel in one or other of this restricted number of orbits. The orbits in question have the peculiar property of always being distant from the nucleus a whole-number multiple of a certain fixed quantity. If the mass of the electron is multiplied by the circumference of its orbit, and the result is again multiplied by its velocity, the result, which is the radius of the orbit, is always expressible as a whole-number multiple of this quantity, twice or three times or four times the quantity, so that one might be justified in supposing that whoever created the physical world thinks in terms of whole numbers. The quantity in question is called Planck's constant. The picture of the atom which I have just sketched is largely due to the work of Sir Ernest Rutherford.

Free Will in the atom.

The atom is not in a constant condition; it may absorb energy from without or radiate energy outwards. When it does the former, an electron jumps from an inner to an outer orbit; when the latter, from an outer to an inner. A peculiar property of these electronic jumps is that the jumping electron does not appear to pass over the intervening space between the orbit of departure and the orbit of arrival. It is simply observed to turn up in a new orbit, having last been observed in a different orbit: so far as the evidence takes us, one might be justified in saying that it goes out of existence in one place and comes into existence again in another. Another peculiar property of the jumps is that we do not know when they will occur or why. They seem, in fact, so far as our knowledge goes at present, to be uncaused. Where a large number of electrons is concerned, we can make a statistical estimate of the proportion of them that will jump over a given period; we also know how far they will jump and what will happen in the neighbourhood of the atom when they do; but we cannot say which particular ones of the number of electrons concerned will do the jumping. 'Each one of these infinitely small units,' said Professor Schrödinger in a recent interview reported in *The Observer*, 'seems to follow its course independently of any determined law. If we can speak of any lawfulness or regularity in such a connection, then lawfulness is merely statistical. It prevails only in the macroscopic realm of the mass,[1] whilst the smallest units follow no rule.'[2]

The behaviour of the electron has suggested to some writers that the motions of the fundamental units of matter may be undetermined. The motions of matter *appear* to be determined only because we normally observe phenomena in the occurrence of which billions of electrons are concerned. The greater the number of electrons concerned, the more certain do statistical estimates of the number which will change their orbits in a given period become; but this does not alter the fact that we are quite unable to say in regard to a particular elec-

---

[1] World of large-scale phenomena; i.e. not the physicist's world.
[2] Schrödinger. Interview with J. W. N. Sullivan. *The Observer*, April 13th, 1930.

tron whether or when it will stray from its orbit, or, if it does, why it does. Individual electrons behave, in other words, as if they possessed spontaneity or free will. This appearance of freedom in the movements of the ultimate constituents of matter is one of the most remarkable features of modern physics; remarkable and disturbing, for it may be made a ground for the suggestion that accident and caprice are at the heart of things, and that order and causation are merely characteristics of the collective appearance of immense numbers of fortuitous happenings observed together. 'Fortuitousness,' on this view, to quote Schrödinger again, 'is the primary state for which there is no plausible explanation, whilst law-fulness only appears in the macroscopic world owing to the co-operation of numerous accidentally operating molecules.'[1]

Professor Schrödinger is not alone among physicists in holding that the movements of matter may be inde-terminate, but he is, perhaps, the most prominent ex-ponent of this view. If he is right, the ultimate happenings in the universe are not predestined, and the fact that we cannot predict the behaviour of individual atoms 'is not a mere practical disability; it is due to the actual nature of things. Thus something like free will is placed at the basis of natural phenomena'.[2] The subject is too difficult, and the bearing upon it of recent advances in physics too obscure, to be discussed here, and I turn to consider the nature of our knowledge of the atom.

How the Atom is known.

How do we know the facts about the atom summarised above? The atom cannot be observed; it is too small. Its existence is inferred from the events which take place in its neighbourhood, which events it is said to cause. Now, so long as the atom remains in a constant state, it

[1] Schrödinger. Interview with J. W. N. Sullivan. *The Observer*, April 13th, 1930.
[2] *ibid.*

has no external effects, and its existence cannot, therefore, be inferred. It is only when an electronic jump occurs, when, that is to say, the atom either absorbs or radiates energy, or when the atom changes in some other way that we know of its existence.

Let us suppose that, as a result of the movement of an electron from an outer to an inner orbit, the atom radiates energy. A series of events will travel outward from the atom like ripples in a pool, which will sooner or later impinge upon objects in their environment producing effects in these objects. These effects in the environment may be observed, and, if they are, we infer that an atom of a certain sort which is giving out energy is responsible for the phenomena observed. Thus we infer the existence of the atom from the effects which it produces, when it changes, in the surrounding neighbourhood. To use a convenient simile of Earl Russell's, let us suppose that a ticket collector is permanently on duty at the exit of the station of a particular town. What will be the nature of his knowledge of the town's population? In the first place, he will only know something about the population when it changes, that is, when somebody enters the town or leaves it. In the second, he will not be aware of these changes where they originally take place, that is in the town itself, but only of the effects of the changes when they manifest themselves at the station. Our knowledge of the atom is of a similarly indirect kind. All that we are really entitled to say is not that we know atoms, but that events in a certain neighbourhood are such as are compatible with and can be calculated on the assumption that there is an electric charge of a certain magnitude in the middle of the neighbourhood. Energy, in fact, spreads outwards from a particular centre. We may, if we like, conceive that there is an arrangement of electrons and protons there which is the source of the energy radiation. But the conception is by no means necessitated. 'The idea that there is a hard lump there, which *is* the electron or proton, is an illegitimate intrusion of common-sense notions derived from touch. For aught we know, the atom may consist entirely of the radiations which come out of it.'[1] Now matter is made of atoms. Matter, therefore, to quote an epigram of Earl Russell's, has become 'a convenient formula for describing what happens where it isn't'.[2]

If the atom resolves itself into the effects which the atom, if it existed, would produce when it changed in the surrounding neighbourhood, what are we to say of the surrounding neighbourhood? Precisely what we have said about the atom. In so far as there are effects in that neighbourhood, they will take the form of occurrences or events. These occurrences or events will be physical. Therefore, they will ultimately be susceptible of the same analysis as that which is applicable to the atom, and will be known only in so far as they produce effects elsewhere. To quote Earl Russell again, 'there is a certain air of taking in each other's washing about the whole business. Events in empty space are only known as regards their abstract mathematical characterisation; matter is only an abstract mathematical characteristic of events in empty spaces'.[3] In other words, we describe what there is at place A in terms of events at places B, C and D; we describe what there is at place B in terms of events at places E, F and G, and so on indefinitely.

The Latest Developments.

Never coming into direct contact with a piece of matter but inferring its existence and character from events elsewhere, which in their turn are inferred from other events which again are inferred from yet other events, and so on *ad infinitum*, it is not to be wondered at that the physicist refrains from dogmatising as to its nature. The picture of the atom as a concrete something conceived as a miniature solar system, is, indeed, only a concession to the incurably pictorial character of our imaginations. In the latest[4] developments of atomic theory, those of Heisenberg

---

[1] Russell. *An Outline of Philosophy*, p. 163.
[2] Russell. *ibid*, p. 165.
[3] Russell. *ibid*, p. 153.
[4] Summer, 1931.

and Schrödinger, the solar-system conception has been given up. There has for long been difficulty in determining whether the atom should be conceived as a small bullet or projectile, or as a system of waves. Some phenomena have seemed to require the former conception; others have been compatible only with the latter. The Rutherford picture of the atom was on the whole a concession to the needs of the projectile point of view; the nucleus was a little accumulation of positive electricity with smaller accumulations of negative electricity embedded in it and rotating round it. But the demands of the phenomena which seem to require a wave motion at the basis of matter have recently re-asserted themselves, and the latest conception transcends the limits of the pictorial imagination by postulating a projectile with wave-like properties and a wave with projectile-like properties. This conception is entailed by the wave-mechanics of de Brogli and Schrödinger. The ultimate particle of matter, presumably the electron, is in this later theory associated with two separate velocities, and each velocity has its special wave-length of corresponding waves. When we remember that the particle is itself a charge of negative electricity which is nevertheless a charge in nothing,[1] we have, it is clear, reached the limits of our imaginative capacity.

Summary.

Into these later complexities we cannot in a book of this kind follow the physicists. Nor, indeed, is it necessary. Atomic theory is in a fluid state and will almost certainly be further modified in the course of the next few years. For our purpose it is sufficient to emphasise two facts. First, the hard, solid basis of matter has disappeared; modern matter is indistinguishable from energy, the source from the emanations which proceed from it. We may, indeed we must, think of the electron as a charge of negative electricity; but the expression is misleading.

[1] See below (next paragraph) for an explanation of this apparent absurdity.

The electron is not something that is charged; it *is* the negative electricity which charges, so that the charge is a charge in nothing but itself. The alternative conception of the basis of matter as consisting of *waves* of energy is, if taken literally, equally misleading. The notion of waves presupposes some medium such as the sea in which the waves may occur, or of which the waves *are* waves. But if the atom is a system of waves, they are waves which are not waves in or of anything.

In the second place, the atom, however we conceive it, is not directly known. Its existence is inferred from events taking place elsewhere which it is presumed to have caused. The observer notices disturbances of a certain sort taking place in a locality. As his observation travels in a particular direction, the disturbances become more marked; at a certain point they reach a maximum intensity. Then they stop. The place at which they stop, the place, in other words, at which nothing is observed to happen, is the place where the atom is. Modern matter is like the grin on the face of the Cheshire cat; the animal has faded away and faded away, until there is only the grin left, with nothing behind to sustain it. Or rather, what is behind we do not know. Hence the way is open for the hypothesis, of which we have already caught sight from another direction, that the phenomena we observe may be merely symbols of a reality which underlies them. The reality, for all we know to the contrary, may be of an entirely different order from the events which symbolise it. It may even be mental or spiritual.

V

C. THE MACHINERY OF PERCEPTION

The problem of perception belongs to philosophy and is exceptionally difficult.[1] The philosophical problem is

[1] Readers who wish to pursue this subject will find a very much fuller treatment in my *Guide to Philosophy*, Chapters I–III (Gollancz, 1936).

not fundamentally altered, still less is it solved, by the discoveries of science, but the knowledge which physics has given us of the properties of light, and the information which physiologists have obtained with regard to the workings of the brain and the nervous system, have enabled it to be treated from a new angle. It is from this angle that I shall approach it. I propose in the first place to summarise the account of the process which a physicist and a physiologist would give. Such a treatment of the subject does not purport to constitute an exhaustive account, although I hope and believe that from the scientific point of view it is correct, so far as it goes.

The Physicist's account of Perception.

Let us suppose that I am a modern physicist who is looking at a distant object. The object I believe to be a highly complicated set of physical processes which are electrical in character. I know further that a physical process, which I call a light ray, starts from the object and travels through the intervening medium of the atmosphere, being changed in the course of its journey into another physical process which ultimately reaches the retina of my eye. Here it is changed into or provokes another physical process which travels along my optic nerve, where it changes into yet another physical process and produces some effect on my brain about which I know very little, but which I assume to be also some kind of physical process. When this final physical process occurs in the brain, there ensues a process of an entirely different kind, namely, a *psychological* process which I call seeing. This is directed not upon the physical process in the brain which was the latest physical effect in the chain of events which preceded it, but upon what is called the object, which I know to be, in fact, a set of complicated physical processes which happened earlier in the series of processes than the brain process, this earlier set of physical processes being selected apparently arbitrarily from among the

chain of physical processes which preceded the occurrence
of the physical process in my brain.

Difficulties in the account.

Now this account is so odd that, whatever the truth of
the matter may be, things cannot, I feel, take place quite
like this. In particular, the account involves a number of
inferences, two of which in particular rest upon assumptions either or both of which may be mistaken. In order
that we may see what these inferences are and what the
assumptions upon which they are based, let us take a
concrete example. Let us suppose that I am looking at a
star, Sirius say, on a dark night. If physics is to be believed, light waves which started to travel from Sirius
many years ago reach (after a specified time which
astronomers calculate) the earth, impinge upon my
retinae and cause me to say that I am seeing Sirius. Now
the Sirius about which they convey information to me is
the Sirius which existed at the time when they started.
This Sirius, may, however, no longer exist; it may have
disappeared in the interim. To say that one can see what
no longer exists is absurd. It follows that, whatever it is
that I am seeing, it is not Sirius. What, in fact, I do see
is a yellow patch of a particular size, shape and intensity.
I infer that this yellow patch had an origin (with which
it is connected by a continuous chain of physical events)
several years ago and many million miles away. But this
inference may be mistaken; the origin of the yellow
patch, which I call a star, may be a blow on the nose, or
a lamp hanging on the mast of a ship.

Nor is this the only inference involved. It is true that
I *think* I am seeing a yellow patch, but am I really justified
in holding this belief? So far as physics and physiology
are concerned, all that we are entitled to say is that the
optic nerve is being stimulated in a certain way, as a
result of which certain events are being caused in the
brain. Are we really justified in saying any more than
this? Possibly we are—the question is really a philosophical

one and this is not the place to offer an opinion upon the issues raised—but it is important to realise that once again an inference is involved, and once again the inference may be mistaken. Directly we go beyond the bare statement 'the optic nerve is being stimulated in such and such a way' and conclude from this fact 'therefore I am seeing an object of such and such a character', we are drawing an inference and are liable to fall into error. What, then, if the physicist and physiologist are right, we in fact know are certain events taking place in our own brains. The outside world is not itself known; its existence is merely an inference due to the fact that we think these events must have a cause.

In a celebrated example Earl Russell cites the case of a physiologist examining the brain of his patient. The physiologist undoubtedly believes himself to be looking at the brain of another person; yet, if Earl Russell, who is provisionally adopting the physicist's point of view, is right, the *cause* of his seeing must be something which is happening in his own. 'Light waves travel from the brain that is being observed to the eye of the physiologist, at which they only arrive after an interval of time, which is finite though short.   The physiologist sees what he is observing only after the light waves have reached his eyes; therefore, the event which constitutes his seeing comes at the end of a series of events which travel from the observed brain to the brain of the physiologist. We cannot, without a preposterous kind of discontinuity, suppose that the physiologist's percept, which comes at the end of this series, is anywhere else but in the physiologist's head.'[1]

When we reflect that, during the period of time which is occupied by the occurrence of the series of events which precede the seeing, the patient's brain may have gone out of existence, the difficulty of supposing that the physiologist is really looking at a brain outside his own becomes very great.

Perception by touch makes the matter even plainer.

[1] Russell. *An Outline of Philosophy*, p. 146.

Suppose that I press my finger against the desk. Ordinarily one would say that there was contact between two material substances. Modern physics, however, as we have seen, lends no countenance to this view. What happens according to the physicist is that repulsion is developed between the atoms composing my finger and those composing the desk. The harder I press the desk, the stronger are the electrical forces which repel my finger. These electrical forces set up in the nerve cell, at the end of my finger a current which reaches my brain, as the result of which I experience the sensation of touching the desk. In fact, however, I am not aware of any object external to my body and, if appropriate parts of my nervous system are suitably stimulated, I shall experience the same sensation of touching the desk, although there is no desk to touch. What is more, I can experience what appears to be a sensation of a pin prick in the non-existent finger of a hand which has been amputated, provided that the nerve terminals in my arm are suitably manipulated.

The External World as Inferred not Perceived.

If we accept the teaching of physics and physiology, what we know in perception are not the movements of matter, but certain events in ourselves connected with those movements; not objects external to ourselves, but the effects of the impact of light-rays and other forms of energy proceeding from these objects upon our bodies.

Professor Eddington is in essentials in agreement with this view of perception. The external world is for him not something that we perceive, but something that we construct from messages that reach the brain along the nerves. The mind, he says, 'weaves an impression out of the stimuli travelling along the nerves to the brain'.[1] Illustrating this conception he makes use of a vivid simile which likens the mind to an editor sitting in his inner

[1] Eddington. *The Nature of the Physical World*, p. 317.

sanctum receiving messages from a number of different reporters and, with the aid of a good deal of invention, piecing them together into a story.[1]

The material which reaches the brain along these channels, the material which the mind must utilise for its story making or world building, is of the scantiest. Colour, temperature, sound, texture, all are lacking. These are not qualities which are given to us from outside, but qualities with which the mind invests the material which reaches it, 'fancies' which it projects into the external world. Even the structure of familiar things, their 'substantiality' and apparent permanence, are bestowed upon them by the mind. For modern physics, as we have seen, has eliminated the notion of substance; chasing it, in Professor Eddington's words, 'from the continuous liquid to the atom, from the atom to the electron', physicists 'have there lost it'.[2] Substance, in fact, is thought to belong to the familiar world only because the mind has put it there. Thus the familiar world is 'subjective' through and through, in the sense that it owes the features which are discerned in it to the activity of the same mind as that which discovers them.

The following quotation embodies the foregoing account of the process of perception in Professor Eddington's own words:

'Consider,' he says, 'how our supposed acquaintance with the lump of matter is attained. Some influence emanating from it plays on the extremity of a nerve starting a series of physical and chemical changes which are propagated along the nerve to a brain cell; there a mystery happens, and an image or sensation arises in the mind which cannot purport to resemble the stimulus which excites it. Everything known about the material world must in one way or another have been inferred from these stimuli transmitted along the nerves. . . . The mind as a central

[1] Eddington. *The Nature of the Physical World*, p. 100.
[2] *ibid*, p. 318.

receiving station reads the dots and dashes of the in-coming nerve-signals. By frequent repetition of their call-signals the various transmitting stations of the outside world become familiar. We begin to feel quite a homely acquaintance with 2LO and 5XX. But a broadcasting station is not *like* its call signal; there is no commensur-ability in their nature. So too the chairs and tables around us which broadcast to us incessantly those signals which affect our sight and touch cannot in their nature be like unto the signals or to the sensations which the signals awake at the end of their journey. . . . It is an astonishing feat of deciphering that we should have been able to infer an orderly scheme of natural knowledge from such in-direct communication.'[1]

What, then, is left in the world outside us? We cannot tell. Once again and by yet another route we are brought to the conclusion, which has already twice been suggested to us, that the world we know, the world not only of the scientist but of everyday life, is a world of symbols. What the symbols symbolise the scientist is no more in a position to say than is the ordinary man.

Mind's Immediate Knowledge of Itself.

But a hint may reach us from another source. There is, as Professor Eddington points out, one kind of knowledge which is exempt from the disabilities which attach to our knowledge of the external world. This is the knowledge which we have of ourselves. 'Clearly,' he says, 'there is one kind of knowledge which cannot pass through such channels, namely, knowledge of the intrinsic nature of that which lies at the far end of the lines of communi-cation.'[2] This knowledge is not a symbolic knowledge of the representations of things, or of the messages which they send us over the telephone lines of nervous com-munication; it is actual knowledge of something as it is

[1] Eddington. *Science and the Unseen World*, pp. 22, 23.
[2] *ibid*, p. 23.

in itself. And this something as it is in itself, the one thing we know directly as it really is, turns out to be mental; it is a mind. 'Mind,' Professor Eddington concludes, 'is the first and most direct thing in our experience; all else is remote inference.' We have, he continues, an acquaintance with the 'mental and spiritual nature of ourselves, known in our minds by an intimate contact transcending the methods of physics'.[1]

In conclusion I will try to indicate some of the suggestions as to the nature of the universe as a whole which modern physicists have put forward on the basis of the considerations outlined above.

VI

REALITY CONCEIVED AS MENTAL OR SPIRITUAL

Idealist tendencies of physics.

Both Sir James Jeans and Professor Eddington have speculated at some length on the implications suggested by the present state of our knowledge of the physical world. Both regard these implications as definitely idealistic; their considered view is that physics suggests that the reality of things is mental or spiritual, and that so-called material phenomena are the effects of the way in which this spiritual reality appears to us. Or, as Eddington would say, material phenomena are the result of abstraction and selection by our minds from the spiritual unity which underlies them.

It is sometimes said that this idealist tendency is peculiar to English physicists. This, however, is not the case. Although the philosophical views of continental physicists are not so well known in this country, it appears that they too subscribe in the main to the general view of mind as fundamental and matter as derivative from mind. This, at least, is true of Einstein, Schrödinger and Planck. 'I

[1] Eddington. *Science and the Unseen World*, p. 24.

regard consciousness as fundamental. I regard matter as derivative from consciousness. We cannot get behind consciousness. Everything that we talk about, everything that we postulate as existing requires consciousness.' So Professor Planck in an interview with J. W. N. Sullivan which appeared in *The Observer*,[1] and the quotation could be paralleled from other reported utterances.

I shall not dwell at length upon these philosophical speculations of modern physicists for two reasons. In the first place, they are not invested with the authority that attaches to the pronouncements of these eminent men of science upon questions which belong properly to their sphere. The philosophic speculations of both Jeans and Eddington are, in fact, on a much lower level than their scientific work, and any competent philosopher could, and many philosophers have subjected their views to damaging criticism.[2]

In the second place, it is not the object of this book either to state or to criticise idealist views of the universe. These can best be studied in philosophical works proper, where systems which affirm the spiritual or mental character of reality are presented with considerable force and worked out in much greater detail than in the concluding chapters of the books of modern physicists. It is sufficient for my purpose to emphasise the fact that the present state of physical knowledge seems to prominent scientists to point to conclusions directly contrary to those of the old materialism, and to favour a spiritual interpretation of the universe as strongly as the science of fifty years ago was thought to favour a materialist interpretation.

In illustration of this contention I propose briefly to summarise a celebrated argument of Sir James Jeans to show that the universe is a thought in the mind of a mathematical thinker.

[1] 25th January, 1931.
[2] See, for example, my *Philosophical Aspects of Modern Science*, Chapters I and II.

Sir James Jeans's concept of a Mathematical Creator.

The steps of Sir James Jeans's argument may be summarised as follows. First, the universe is more easily analysable in terms of mathematical concepts than of those appropriate to any other science. The further we penetrate into the nature of physical things the more plainly are the mathematical principles underlying them laid bare. Substantial matter, as we have seen, is in modern physics gradually shredded away; structure and relations only are left. Structure and relations are expressible in terms of mathematical formulae. The universe in short is more like a mathematical formula than it is like a machine, a living organism, a moral concept or a work of art.

Secondly, our mathematical knowledge has been, as it were, spun out of our own minds. We have not achieved it by studying the workings of nature and then deducing general mathematical truths from what we have observed. We have discovered that three cubed is twenty-seven and that the square on the hypotenuse of a right-angled triangle is equal to the sum of the squares on the other two sides by following the operations of our reasons and then reflecting upon their implications. Having formulated the laws of mathematics for ourselves, we turn our attention to the things of the outside world and find that they obey them. This is a very surprising fact. Considering our insignificance in the universe, there is no reason why we should expect to find ourselves capable of understanding its operations. The most likely supposition would be that the universe should be meaningless to us. In fact, however, it is found to obey precisely the same laws as those which we ourselves have formulated. It is as if, having drawn up the rules of a game for ourselves, we found that everything in the universe was playing according to our rules.

What is the significance of this fact? First, that our own minds and the external world both originate in the constructive operations of the same mind. If that is in fact the case, that they should both work in accordance with the same laws is exactly what we would expect. Secondly, we are justified in drawing an inference as to the nature of this constructing mind; it must think or be capable of thinking mathematically.

The Beginning of the Universe.

Now, Sir James Jeans elsewhere makes use of a number of facts derived from modern astronomy to prove that the universe came into being as the result of an act of creation. These facts are connected with the principle of entropy. Entropy means wastage or diffusion, and many astronomers, including Sir James Jeans, are inclined to the view that the universe is wasting away; it is like a clock that is running down. The heavier atoms radiate away their substance in the form of radiant energy, and break down into lighter atoms (the 'burnt-out ash' of which the stuff of our planet is composed). Sir James Jeans is responsible for the theory that in the centre of the stars the heat is so intense that protons and electrons are actually annihilated; it is this annihilation of protons and electrons which he regards as the source of the recently discovered phenomena known as cosmic rays or cool radiation. Everywhere these processes of annihilation and breaking down are going on and there is, Sir James Jeans holds, no known example of the contrary process.[1] 'The transformation of matter into radiation is a "one-way", or, as it is technically called, an irreversible process. Matter can change into radiation, but under present conditions radiation can never change back into matter.'[2]

Ultimately, therefore, the fate of the universe is 'to dissolve into radiation; there would be neither sunlight nor starlight but only a cool glow of radiation uniformly diffused through space.'[3]

[1] Professor Milliken has put forward a theory which ascribes cosmic rays to a *building-up* process; but Sir James Jeans does not accept this view.
[2] Sir James Jeans. *Eos*, p. 52.   [3] *ibid*, p. 56.

Since the universe bears witness only to processes of energy diffusion, some other process must be postulated for the concentration of the energy diffused. To put the point pictorially, the processes known to cosmic physics are analogous to the gradual diffusion of a drop of ink in a glass of water; an observer of this diffusion would infer that somebody had shaken the drop into the water. Similarly, Sir James Jeans infers an act or series of acts of energy-storing or energy-concentration in the form of matter, which he envisages as acts of creation. 'Everything,' he says, 'points with overwhelming force to a definite event, or series of events, of creation at some time or times, not infinitely remote. The universe cannot have originated by chance out of its present ingredients, and neither can it always have been the same as now.'[1]

The Universe as a thought in God's mind.

We have thus established both the need for a creator and the fact that he is capable of mathematical thinking. The further step, which consists in showing that the universe is a thought in his mind, is not so clear as could be wished; nor is the argument one which can be easily summarised. It consists of two main stages. First, it is asserted that any phenomenon in the world studied by physics is exhaustively analysable in terms of mathematics. This means, presumably, that when you have given a complete mathematical account of it, when you have said all about it that a mathematician theoretically could say, there is nothing left to say at all. And there is nothing left to say at all because there is nothing left to say it about; for the mathematical properties of a thing are, on this view, all the properties that it has; in other words, a thing *is* its mathematical properties. Just as the atom resolved itself into the sum of the changes in the surrounding neighbourhood which the atom would produce, if it existed, so an exhaustively complete mathematical account of a thing may be described as an account of the properties

[1] Sir James Jeans. *Eos,* p. 55.

which would be regarded as the mathematical properties of the thing, if there were a thing to have the properties. Once again, as so often in modern physics, we are asked to conceive of laws and formulas which there is nothing left to obey, of the 'grin' of the Cheshire cat without the cat. The paradox arises from the fact that the laws and formulas have now been pushed so far that there is nothing outside and beyond them to conform to them. Science having eliminated substances can only describe the effects of hypothetical substances. It is these effects which are completely describable in terms of mathematics, and, the task accomplished, the hypothetical substance which was supposed to have the effects is dropped.

Secondly, to be mathematical is to be mental. Mathematics is a system of the thoughts of a mind, a system which, we have seen, Sir James Jeans believes to have been discovered by human minds reflecting upon the implications of their own modes of working. The laws of mathematics, admittedly, purport to apply to things out there in the world; but they are not themselves out there in the world; they are in our minds. Now to say that physics has got rid of substance, is to say that physics has got rid of 'things out there in the world'. The laws which would have been applied to them, had they existed (again the grin without the cat), are all that is left, and these laws are mental.

Hence we reach the conclusion that the universe is a universe of thought; it is a thought in the mind of a mathematical thinker. The apparent objectivity of things, says Sir James Jeans, is due to their 'subsisting in the mind of some eternal spirit';[1] and so we reach a complete Idealism in the adoption of the 'concept of the universe as a world of pure thought'.[2]

I have summarised Sir James Jeans's account in some little detail because it typifies the tendency of modern physics to introduce a distinction between the appearance

[1] Sir James Jeans. *The Mysterious Universe* p. 137.
[2] *ibid*, p. 140.

of things and their reality. The appearance of things is material; it is an appearance of chairs and tables, or of atoms and electrons, according to the nature of the inspection we bring to bear upon it. But the reality is other than the appearance. Hence, scientific knowledge is not knowledge of reality but of appearance.

VII

INTUITIONAL KNOWLEDGE CONTRASTED WITH SCIENTIFIC

How, then, do we know the reality? An answer which is frequently given in current, scientific thought is that we know it by means of an intuitional faculty which, unlike the scientific reason, gives us *direct* knowledge. The scientific reason, as we have seen, abstracts and selects; moreover, it does not, it is said, give us information about things in themselves but about symbols, symbols for whose construction it is itself in part responsible.

But we have other kinds of knowledge besides the knowledge which science gives; there is the knowledge which we have of ourselves, there is our knowledge of right or beauty, there is the knowledge which is involved in seeing a joke or in understanding a person's character. To suppose that we can only know a thing as a scientist knows it is to be guilty of a very elementary blunder. The following examples indicate what is meant by intuitional as specifically contrasted with scientific knowledge.

The Scientific account of hearing a Bach fugue.

Let us take first the processes involved in the appreciation of a piece of music, say a Bach fugue. What account does science give of these processes? Bach, presumably, conceived a musical idea (the ambiguity of this expression must be pardoned; I am not here concerned with the true interpretation of the aesthetic process) as a result of

which a message travelled along the neural fibres
running down his arm to his finger-tips, as a result of
which certain forces of electrical attraction and repulsion
were set in motion between the atoms constituting the
extreme ends of his finger-tips and those constituting
the keys of, let us say, a harpsichord. Strings were plucked
and waves travelled out into the atmosphere and impinged
upon Bach's eardrums. The eardrums were caused to
vibrate and the vibrations travelling through the middle
ears reached the cochleas of the inner ears. Here they
caused certain wave-like disturbances in the fluids
contained in the cochleas, as a result of which the cilia,
long hairs ranged along the inner bones of the cochleas,
were swayed to and fro; the motion of the swaying cilia
transmitted certain neural impulses to Bach's brain, as
the result of which, or partly as the result of which, he
experienced the *psychological* sensation of hearing the music.
Presuming that he approved of what he heard, we may
suppose him to have made a series of black marks upon
white paper—the score. This procedure would again
involve a whole set of complicated physical processes,
some of which physiologists, neurologists and physicists
would be able to analyse. The score is copied and re-
copied until some two hundred years afterwards somebody reads it—a complicated set of visual, neural
processes being thereby involved—plays it, thereby
setting in motion electrical atomic processes similar to
those indicated above, and causing a succession of sound-
waves to travel through the atmosphere. These, impinging
upon the eardrums, stimulate the machinery of cochlea,
cilia and so forth, with the result that I in my turn experience the sensation of hearing the music.

The various processes to which I have referred could
be described in much greater detail, and I have mentioned only a few of those that are involved. To give a
complete account of all the events which take place
between the moment at which Bach conceived the
musical idea and that at which I hear a Bach fugue

D

would probably fill a volume. But of the one thing that matters, the beauty of the music, no word would have been said; nor would any account have been given of the pleasure which I experience in the hearing of it, or of why I experience that pleasure. If I say that the fugue is beautiful and that the appreciation of beauty gives pleasure, the scientist will reply, 'Very likely, but I know nothing of that.'

Science, moreover, is unable to suggest any reason why the fugue should be beautiful. The statement of the theme of a Bach fugue consists normally of not more than a dozen notes. To strike these notes at random upon a piano is to start a chain of physical processes, of the nature and apprehension of which the physicist and the physiologist between them might give a reasonably satisfactory account. It would be satisfactory in the sense that it would include everything of importance that there was to say about them. Arrange the same notes in such a way as to form the statement of the fugue's theme, and, hearing them, you may be thrilled to ecstasy. The actual physical and physiological events that occur, the sound waves that travel through the atmosphere, the vibrations in the eardrums, are the same in both cases; it is only their sequence which is different. The order and sequence of the physical events is, in other words, an essential ingredient in the occurrence and appreciation of value; yet order and sequence are not themselves physical things and no account of them, therefore, can be given in scientific terms.

The Scientist's Account of a Joke.

A second example may be cited from the case of humour. The following instance from Sir Arthur Eddington admirably illustrates the point at issue. What, Eddington asks, is the nature of the activity involved in the seeing of a joke? He points out that a joke, like a chemical compound, can be subjected to analysis, dissected into its component parts and, after careful examination of them, pronounced to be truly a member of the species 'joke'. Having made sure of the fact, having convinced oneself that this is an authentic specimen of humour, the next step logically should be to laugh. But this, he points out, is just what in the circumstances in question we should not do. For in the process of scrutiny and classification the quality that really makes it a joke, its laughableness, has been destroyed. It evaporated when we analysed the joke into its component parts; nor can it be re-created by putting the parts together again.[1]

Two conclusions emerge: first, the important thing about a joke, its laughableness, is a quality of a whole; secondly, the method by which this quality is known is not the method of science. The method of science is to classify and to analyse, but the way to know a joke is to have a sense of humour.

Summary of Preceding Arguments.

We are now in a position to put together the preceding lines of argument and to draw our conclusions. First, the method of science is not the only method of knowing things. Secondly, there are some things, beauty, for example, and humour, of which science is unable to give any account; yet these things are intensely important to us. Thirdly, in so far as these things are known, it must be by some faculty other than scientific observation and reasoning. Fourthly, we have seen reason to suppose that the world that science studies is not the real world but a selected or abstracted aspect of something that underlies it. This 'something other' is not and cannot be known by the methods of science. It is plausible, therefore, to suppose that it is known by some method analogous to that by which we know beauty in art and humour in jokes. But just as we can describe neither beauty nor humour, so it is unfair to expect those who do in fact have knowledge of this reality that underlies the world of science to give a logical account of it.

[1] Eddington. *The Nature of the Physical World*, p. 322.

If we ask, then, how the reality is to be conceived, it is probable that we shall get a number of different answers varying with the personality of the answerer. It is a mathematician's mind according to Sir James Jeans, a universal mind-stuff according to Professor Eddington, an organic unity rather like a person according to Professor Whitehead, a stream of force of life according to Bergson.

To this reality the approach is not through science, but through art, through the appreciation of nature, and above all through religion.

VIII

CONCLUSIONS

Without further following the thinkers with whose theories we have been concerned into these speculative regions, in which private conviction and personal experience are apt to take the place of public argument and reasoned demonstration, we may, in the light of the considerations advanced in this chapter, safely affirm four conclusions of a general character to which most modern writers on science would, I think, subscribe.

First, scientific research in physics and chemistry is not a process whereby the mind explores a world of matter existing independently of itself. Scientific thought is an activity which substantially affects the nature of that which it studies. It abstracts, classifies, analyses, takes to bits, and, in so doing, it modifies, if it does not actually destroy, the concrete reality with which it purports to deal.

Secondly, physics is, therefore, to some extent subjective. It used to be urged that psychology, regarded as the study of mind, was not and never could be scientific, for the reason that the only mind to which the psychologist had access was his own. By introspection, it was thought, he could acquaint himself with its contents. But the mind which he introspected was the same as the mind by means of which the introspecting was being performed; it was, therefore, necessarily affected by the fact that it was being made the object of inquiry, with the result that it was extraordinarily difficult for the psychologist to avoid finding what he expected to find. It now appears that physics is in much the same plight. For the subject-matter of physics, like that of psychology, is modified and moulded by the mental activity involved in its exploration. The inference is, as Mr. Joseph Needham puts it, that 'the world as seen by science is not the world as it really is.'[1] It used to be thought that physics was a process of discovery or exploration, whereby the external world was by a sort of revelation revealed to the mind of the enquiring physicist. But, to quote again from Mr. Needham, 'the concept of Revelation has been removed from science.'[2]

Hence, the suggestion now made in many quarters that science is essentially a form of art. It is an imaginative picture constructed by the human mind of the workings of the universe, not, as it used to be thought, a photographic representation. And, inevitably, the picture will bear upon it the imprint of the personality of the artist. This is the view of their activities which many eminent scientists seem increasingly disposed to take. 'I found that not only Einstein, but also Planck and Schrö-dinger fully recognised the subjective element in science. Planck in particular . . . regards science as a constructed work of art, expressing a certain side of man's nature.'[3]

Thirdly, science does not tell us the whole truth about things. It only provides us with partial truths about those aspects of things which it has selected for treatment because they are amenable to its methods. It used to be customary to divide subjects into those with which science

---

[1] Needham. *The Sceptical Biologist*, p. 245.
[2] Needham. *The Sceptical Biologist*, p. 61.
[3] Interviews with Eminent Scientists. By J. W. N. Sullivan. *Observer*, 13th April, 1930.

was competent to deal, and those, such as music, or religion, with which it was not. This division is misleading. Science is competent to tell us something about everything; but it cannot tell us the whole truth about anything. Moreover, in regard to many things the information which it has to offer is not the kind of information which matters.[1] Hence, the mechanist theory of the world, although it may give us important information about the way in which things behave, is no longer regarded as containing the exclusive truth about the world.

Fourthly, there are avenues for the exploration of the universe other than that of science, notably through the aesthetic, the moral and the religious consciousnesses. These avenues are not only as valid as the approach through science; they may be even more important, since while, as we have seen, science does not give us information about the reality of things, or rather about the reality behind them, art and religion may do so. Some scientists indeed, for example, Schrödinger, seem to regard science as a comparatively unimportant means of access to reality. 'In the new universe, it appears, our religious insight is granted as great validity as our scientific insight. Indeed, in the opinion of the greatest creator of them all (Einstein) our religious insight is the source and guide of our scientific insight.'[2] This is not to say that science, which formerly was thought to disprove religion, now supports it; merely it no longer affords any reason for thinking it to be untrue. It may supplement but no longer contradicts the deliverances of the religious consciousness. Science in fact has cleared the boards of the universe for religion, but it has no contribution to make to the writing of the play.

[1] For a fuller account of the significance of the knowledge obtained by science and of the nature and limitations of scientific method, see my *Philosophy For Our Times* (Nelson 1940).

[2] Interviews with Eminent Scientists. By J. W. N. Sullivan. *Observer*, 13th April, 1930.

CHAPTER V

CURRENT THEORIES OF LIFE AND MATTER

Author's Bias.

This chapter and the next must be prefaced with a note of warning. Of all the chapters in the book they most nearly represent the views of the writer. It may, therefore, well be the case that the standard of impartiality, which I have endeavoured to observe throughout this book, is not maintained; that I have attributed importance to theories less because they are current than because they are mine, and suggest trains of argument which are invested with no greater authority than the approval of the writer and have no origin save in his own mind. It is well for all parties that this warning should be borne in mind; it testifies to frankness in the author and induces caution in the reader.

We have seen in the last chapter how materialism has broken down in physics. We have now to consider how it has fared in the realm of biology. Here, too, the history of recent thought has been largely the history of its super-session; in fact, the nineteenth-century view has been largely abandoned, but the abandonment has been less spectacular than in physics, and the evidence which has been responsible for it is neither so positive nor so un-assailable as that which was considered in the last chapter.

There has been a growing realisation that something more than the materialist hypothesis is required to account for the development and evolution of life and the difference in behaviour between living organisms and non-living matter. This realisation has in its turn generated a number of theories which, seeking to interpret the peculiar character and behaviour of life, and originating, therefore, in the realm of biology, tend to take on a philosophical sweep and scope, so that from being theories of evolution they develop into theories of the universe. I will first consider very briefly the nature of the evidence which has led to the gradual supersession of the view of evolution as a purely mechanical process, and, secondly, outline some contemporary views with regard to the nature of the universe as a whole, which have been chiefly inspired by biology.

I

CRITICISMS OF MECHANISM IN BIOLOGY

Characteristic Behaviour of Living Organisms.

'Though the physico-chemical, or mechanistic conception of life is still very much alive in the minds of popular writers, I think it is now far from being so among serious students of biology.'[1] This statement appears at the beginning of Professor J. S. Haldane's series of Donnellan lectures delivered in the University of Dublin in the spring of 1930. He proceeds to cite as one of the grounds for this assertion the fact that 'from the standpoint of the physical sciences the maintenance and reproduction of a living organism is nothing less than a standing miracle, and for the reason that coordinated maintenance of structure and activity is inconsistent with the physical conception of self-existent matter and energy.'[2]

Two rather different conceptions are emphasised in the succeeding lectures. In the first place, living organisms exhibit what can only be represented as an inner drive to reach their appropriate form and structure, and, when it is reached, to maintain it. In the second, they exhibit a similar drive to reach and maintain the environment appropriate to their proper functioning.

An obvious illustration of the first conception is the behaviour of a crab who, when its leg is knocked off, proceeds to grow another. Inventors have yet to fashion a machine which will spontaneously replace a lost or damaged part with a new one. A more striking example

[1-2] J. S. Haldane. *The Philosophical Basis of Biology*, p. 12.

is afforded by the experiments of the German biologist Driesch.

In Driesch's experiments an embryo which has reached the stage in which it is a hollow sphere of undifferentiated cells without top or bottom, right or left, was divided into two or more sections by sharp cuts. Driesch found that each section developed into a complete embryo. Since the cuts might have been made along an almost infinite number of planes, any one part of the embryo must, it would seem, be prepared to assume any function and to develop any characteristics; it must also be credited with an unconscious knowledge of how the other parts are developing. Thus any one cell can become a liver cell, a blood corpuscle, or a piece of bone tissue, according to the needs of the organism as a whole. 'A very strange sort of machine, indeed,' says Driesch, 'which is the same in all its parts.' 'It is not possible,' he continues, 'to conceive of a machine being divided in any direction and still remaining a machine.'[1]

Driesch was led to the conclusion that there is a spontaneous tendency or drive in the organism to reach its appropriate form-structure and perform its appropriate function, in spite of interference, provided that the interference is not too great. The suggestion follows that it is only by considering the organism as a unity, a unity which can be regarded as the vehicle of this drive or force, even, it may be, of something analogous to an intention, that facts of this kind can be interpreted.

Quest of Appropriate Environment.

As an example of the second conception, the drive to achieve and to maintain the environment appropriate to the creature's activities, take the case of the salmon proceeding up-stream, leaping obstacles and breasting the current in order to deposit her spawn in a particular environment. To suggest that the salmon is the vehicle of

[1] Quoted in *Science, Religion and Reality*: edited by Joseph Needham, p. 236. See for further examples Chapter VII, pp. 188, 189.

an unconscious purpose to reach this appropriate environment, a purpose which impels it to go on acting in a
particular way until it succeeds, since it is to postulate
more than can be observed, is also to postulate more than
can be proved and more than a materialist would be prepared to allow. Yet it is extraordinarily difficult to explain
the salmon's behaviour on any other assumption. It acts
exactly *as if* it were so impelled. Under the influence of
what is apparently an unconscious purpose to reach and
maintain the environments which are appropriate to
them, organisms will alter not only their behaviour but
their structure. Thus, if you take the hydroid plant
antennularia and remove it from the flat surface to which
it is accustomed to adhere, it will immediately begin to
change its structure, proliferating long waving roots or
fibres in the vain effort to find something to grip. So,
too, with the hyacinth bulbs which are commonly placed
in jars. There is, in other words, in these cases a definite
attempt on the part of the organism to adapt itself, if
necessary by altering its structure, to an abnormal environment. Examples could, of course, be multiplied
indefinitely.

Professor Haldane arrived at similar conclusions from
an examination of the delicately adjusted responses of the
living organism to variations in oxygen supply.

The Active Response of the Living Organism.

On the basis of these and similar considerations two
principles emerge, each of which is incompatible with a
strictly mechanist interpretation.

(i) In the first place, the behaviour of an organism cannot in all cases be adequately interpreted in terms of response to the stimulus of the environment. It is in this
respect that its difference from a machine is most manifest. The responses of machines to their environment are
automatic. Wind the spring and the watch goes; turn the
handle and the engine starts. But the response of a living
organism to a stimulus, if response it can be called, is active.

In this activity of response biologists and psychologists have traditionally distinguished three phases. (a) There is a perception of an external situation. The salmon sees the rocks over which it must leap. This perception may lead merely to a number of external movements, as in the case of the salmon, or to an alteration in structure of a permanent kind, as in the case of the *antennularia*.

(b) There is what psychologists call a conation, that is to say, a strong impulse of the same instinctive type as those which prompt us to maintain and reproduce the species by eating and making love. Such impulses and the activities that spring from them appear to be partially independent of any change in or stimulus from the external environment. The important point is that the extent of a creature's activity or response will depend not only upon the amount of stimulus applied, but also upon the intensity of his conative impulse. The conative impulse is, in short, an additional and an intermediate factor between stimulus and response, which the machine does not possess; it is because of it that the response of the living creature is regarded as an *active* response.

(c) There is purposive activity directed to a definite end, and continuing after the stimulus has ceased to be applied. A machine stops when it has run down. The salmon continues to leap in its endeavour to overcome the rocks, until it succeeds.

One way of putting the conclusion that emerges is that, whereas in the case of a machine interaction with the environment is a one-way process, causation proceeding always from the environment to the machine, in the case of the living organism the process is a two-way process, the organism moulding and adapting the environment to itself just as the environment moulds and adapts the organism. Professor Haldane, indeed, has gone so far as to maintain that the proper unit for biological investigation is not the living organism at all, but the organism plus its environment. 'The conception of life,' he says, 'embraces the environment of an organism, as well as what is *within* its body.'[1] The organism cannot, that is to say, in his view, be treated in isolation as a unit divorced from its environment; it is so closely bound up with the environment, the coordination of the two is so complete, that it is only as constituting conjointly with the environment a single unit that it can be adequately considered.

In any event we are led to the conception of the organism as a vehicle of spontaneous energy, in virtue of which it moulds and affects, as well as is moulded and affected by its surroundings.

The Organism as a Whole.

(ii) In the second place, whatever view we may take of this rather difficult conception of the organism as forming together with its environment a whole, the view of the organism as being itself in some sense a whole is more or less necessitated. The word 'whole' here is used in a technical sense to mean something which is more than the sum of its parts. As such, a whole is to be distinguished from an aggregate. A machine is an aggregate. It is, that is to say, simply the assembly of its parts, the arithmetical sum total of all the cranks and nuts and screws which it may be found to contain. You can take a machine to pieces, examine each of its component parts separately and put them together again. Or, if you like, you can arrange them differently so that they form another machine.

A living body is not susceptible of this treatment. The days are long past when a man was able to regard his body as ' a system of pipes and tubes', in Addison's phrase, reacting like any other pipes and tubes to what was put into and taken out of them. A body is admittedly a collection of pipes and tubes, but it is also something more than that. It is, in other words, a whole or a unity, the distinction between a whole and an aggregate being that, whereas an aggregate is merely the sum of its parts, a whole is more than the sum of its parts. It is something over and above them, brought into being by their coming together,

[1] Haldane. *The Philosophical Basis of Biology*, p. 18.

but not, therefore, to be resolved into them. Thus an organ in the body is not an isolated, separable entity existing in its own right; it is a component part of a whole, and is bound by necessary relations both to the whole and to all the other organs which compose the whole. Divested of these relations, taken, that is to say, as an isolated entity divorced from the rest of the body, the organ would not be the organ that it is; it would be quite literally something different. Hence, when it is said that the body is a whole or unity, one of the things that is meant is that its parts owe their nature to the fact of their being parts of the whole, that they are bound by necessary relations to the other parts, and that they form together with these other parts and with the relations a new entity, namely, the whole body, which can only be broken up at the cost of the destruction of the parts as parts. You cannot, in short, take a living creature to pieces and put him together again as you can do in the case of a machine, nor can you rearrange his parts so as to make a different creature; and you cannot do these things for the simple reason that by taking him to pieces you would not merely disperse an aggregate but would destroy a whole.

The 'Hormic' Psychology.

It is to its neglect of this feature of the wholeness or unity of the organism that the plausibility of mechanism is said to be due. It is, in fact, the case that, if you consider the working of each of the parts of an organism separately, the organism appears to function as a machine. But in addition to the separate functionings of the separate parts, there is the reciprocal influence of the parts upon each other. This reciprocal influence takes the form of an apparently spontaneous cooperation by the parts to promote the welfare of the organism. The so-called 'hormic' psychology, a development of the last few years, regards the human organism as a combination of living elements, both bodily and mental, all of which cooperate together for the good of the organism, but each of which retains some measure of vital initiative in virtue of which it may pursue courses different from and even antagonistic to those of the whole. This conception of the independent action of different living units in the body is sufficiently familiar in connection with the behaviour of the phago-cytes or white corpuscles in the blood. These cooperate with the rest of the organism in surrounding and digesting intruding bacteria; the cooperation, however, is not auto-matic or inevitable, but is one of voluntary and indepen-dent units, each of which, in Professor Graham Wallas's words, 'hunts and digests nearly as independently as if it were an isolated inhabitant of a warm tropical sea'.

'A man's hair,' he continues, 'cooperates with the rest of his organism by protecting his brain from blows and from sudden changes of temperature, but it may go on growing though the man has ceased to live. His epithelial cells may begin at any moment to proliferate indepen-dently, and so cause death by cancer. Red blood cor-puscles or patches of skin transferred from one man to another may both continue their own activities and also cooperate in the wider functions of the new organism of which they are now parts.'[1]

Now this cooperation of apparently independent parts seems to require the conception of wholeness described above; it requires, in other words, that the life of the organism should be regarded as a whole. For, while each part performs its separate function, which is necessary to the maintenance of the life of the whole organism, the activity by means of which their mutual cooperation is achieved is not itself the activity of any part. The con-clusion is that 'we must', in Professor Haldane's words, 'regard (living) phenomena as being, in so far as we under-stand them at all, the active manifestation of a persistent whole; and the whole is what we call the life of the organism.'[2]

[1] Wallas. *The Art of Thought*, p. 37.
[2] Haldane. *The Philosophical Basis of Biology*, p. 18.

These considerations reinforce the view of the living organism as the expression of an active drive or impulsion modifying its environment, coordinating the environment with itself, coordinating its own cooperating parts and developing by and through such activity and coordination.

The Persistence of Evolution.

One further consideration derived from the biological sphere, may be mentioned here, because of its bearing upon the mechanist theory. This consideration has been advanced by the French philosopher, Bergson. Let us assume, he says in effect, that the only motive force of the process of evolution is that adaptation of the organism to environment upon which Lamarck laid stress. The organism, according to this view, is a very delicately adjusted machine which automatically responds to changes in the environment by adapting itself to them; or, if it does not, it perishes in the struggle for existence through its failure to adapt.

Why, then, asks Bergson, if this account of the matter be correct, did not the process of evolution stop? Considered merely by the standard of the degree of *physical* adaptation achieved—and on the mechanist-materialist view we are only entitled to speak of *physical* adaptation, since only the physical is real—many of the species which evolution has thrown up in the past are better adapted to their environment than is man. The monkey, for example, suffers from fewer diseases, the elephant is longer lived than man. The tiger has succeeded in evolving a covering which renders him immune from the vagaries of the climate, and kills only as many of his fellow creatures as he requires for his sustenance. Man, considered from the purely physical point of view, is ridiculously unfitted to his environment, so much so that he is unable to exist, unless he is protected from it by coverings taken from other animals. His body is delicate, unnecessarily complicated, and easily put out of order, for example, by food which other animals assimilate without difficulty; moreover, it is a prey to innumerable diseases. Why, then, if the motive force and driving power behind evolution is the need to secure adaptation to environment, did not evolution stop at the elephant and the monkey? Why did it go on to produce man? Is it possible to resist the conclusion that evolution is the expression of some force which, not content with achieving relative safety for its creatures by adapting them to their environment, proceeds to complicate itself ever more and more dangerously, in the endeavour to evolve *higher* forms of life?

But, in using the words 'higher forms of life' and postulating a purposive drive on the part of evolution to achieve them, our treatment is moving outside the purely physical sphere in which matter alone exists, and introducing the notions of comparative values and of purpose to realise those which are higher. These conceptions in their turn presuppose the existence of a principle which is not a material principle, whose operations must be taken into consideration in any satisfactory account of the process of evolution.

II

PHILOSOPHICAL THEORIES BASED ON BIOLOGY

Prevalence of Idealist Views.

Assuming the necessity for the introduction of some principle or activity other than and in addition to the material stuff of which the earth and the bodies of living organisms seem to be composed, how are we to envisage it? Clearly it must be non-material; if it were merely a form of matter, the universe would be composed exclusively of matter, and we should be thrown back upon the necessity of explaining everything that happens or exists exclusively in terms of the movements of atoms and electrons. If it is not material, we must, presumably, conceive it after the model of mind.

Interpretations of the universe in terms of mind have

frequently been put forward by idealist philosophers. Idealism is, on the whole, the dominant strain in philosophy and the thorough-going explanations of the universe in terms of mind which the various forms of Idealism have worked out, have seemed to many to be not less convincing, as they are certainly more all-embracing, than those which have been advanced on any other basis.

As I pointed out in the last chapter, the tendency of modern physics is undoubtedly idealistic, and certain philosophers, notably the late Professor Wildon Carr, have acclaimed recent developments in our knowledge of the so-called physical world as affording contributory evidence of the independently established truth of Idealism. Moreover, an important modern school of Idealism, known as neo-Idealism, flourishes in Italy under the leadership of Croce and Gentile, which insists that the universe must be interpreted in terms of mind, a view which is favoured on the ground that it is not only consonant with but required by the science of the times. In general, however, idealist theories, although their acceptance may of recent years have owed something to the trend of science, are advocated on grounds unconnected with science. For this reason they do not properly fall within the scope of this book, which is chiefly concerned to estimate the influence upon current thought of developments in our scientific knowledge.

To affirm that the additional principle or activity which modern biology seems to demand must be conceived after the model of mind does not take us very far. The word 'mental' is an ambiguous expression covering many types of occurrence, from the intellectual activities of the mathematician and the spiritual vision of the saint to the erotic longings of the savage or the smell sensations of the dog. Mind, moreover, may be in its essential nature unconscious, or the conscious aspect of something that is normally unconscious but rises into consciousness only rarely and under certain favourable conditions. Mind on this latter view is a particular form of life; it is life as it appears at a certain level of evolution, and life will in its essential values be conceived as an urge or impulsion, normally unconscious but achieving consciousness in certain rather exceptional individual expressions of itself. It is to a force or stream of life which, receiving its most typical, although not its highest, expression in the simple cravings and urges of the lower animals, appears at its highest in the self-conscious ratiocinating mind that, in the view of many, the facts of biology seem to point.

Two alternative possibilities here present themselves. Either this force or stream of life exists side by side with matter, so that the universe may be supposed to contain at least two fundamentally different kinds of entities, or, as I should prefer to call them, two different principles; or the force or stream of life is all that there is, so-called inorganic matter being regarded as an illusion.

The Universe as a dynamic flux of change.

The second hypothesis has been elaborated by the philosopher Bergson in a celebrated book, *Creative Evolution*. His theory is philosophical rather than biological, an account of the universe rather than of evolution; but it is an account of the universe in terms of evolution, and it seeks to explain all the richness and variety of the world, the movements of the tides no less than the desires of the lover, the formation of the rocks as well as the thought of the philosopher, in terms of the expression of a single all-pervasive vital stream. This vital stream, the *élan vital*, which is for Bergson the fundamental stuff of the universe, is conceived after the model of our own consciousness, of our consciousness not as rational and intellectual, but as instinctive and intuitive. The one permanent and inalienable characteristic of the *élan vital* is constant change. The universe, says Bergson, is a universe of change, and the continual flow which is our own consciousness, the thrust and play of changing impulse, thought and feeling which is the stuff of human experience, is the key to the interpretation of the world, the model after which we are asked to conceive of the universe as a whole. Bergson has shown very great ingenuity in explaining everything that exists in terms of the continuous thrust and pulse of this everflowing stream of reality.

The exposition of his view is technical and cannot be pursued here.[1] It is, however, open to serious objections, more particularly in regard to its account of matter. If the universe consists exclusively of the *élan vital*, which is a flow of change, matter, it is clear, must be an illusion. Bergson explains this illusion as due to the operations of the intellect. The intellect is a faculty which, he holds, has been evolved in the course of evolution for purely practical purposes. Life in a world of undifferentiated change would offer serious difficulties. Hence, the intellect has been evolved; its function is to make 'cuts across the living flow', introducing divisions and distinctions into what is fundamentally a continuous flux of change. As a result of these divisions and distinctions the world appears to us as a collection of solid, static objects extended in space, as, in short, a world of matter. But these objects have been carved out of the flux by the intellect; they do not exist independently of it. Hence, in conceiving of reality as the intellect leads us for practical purposes to picture it we fall, in Bergson's view, into error. For the intellect does not provide us with the real truth about things, which is reached by another faculty called by Bergson 'intuition'.

Criticism of Bergson.

We here meet in a new form the familiar distinction between appearance and reality. The universe is *really* a world of continuous change without division or distinction; it only *appears* as objects extended in space. To this account it may be objected that, if the intellect is free to introduce whatever distinctions it likes in a fundamentally homogeneous world, we ought to be able to

[1] For an account of Bergson's Philosophy see my *Introduction to Modern Philosophy*. World's Manuals (O.U.P.), Chapter V.

carve out from the flux of reality what objects we please. If this is so, it is a little difficult to understand why we should not carve out only such as please us, why, in fact, we should carve out missed trains and dentists' drills. Facts exist which undoubtedly thwart our wishes and impede our activities. It is a little hard to be told that we have deliberately made these facts for ourselves. The best definition of Heaven I know is a place in which all the facts are such as we should wish them to be, and it looks, therefore, as if it is only in Heaven that Bergson's philosophy is true.

If, on the other hand, reality is not really featureless and homogeneous, then the divisions and distinctions between things are not *made* but *found* by the intellect, and the familiar differences between one thing and another creep back in another form. They are really *there*, and it is not an illusion of the intellect that makes us *think* them there. Moreover, if the intellect does not give us truth, we may well ask why we should accept Bergson's account of the universe as true. This account is highly intellectual; it is supported by rational arguments designed to appeal to the reasons of others and presented with considerable intellectual force. But, if the intellect is misleading when taken as a guide to the real nature of things, the arguments which are advanced to show that it is, in so far as they are intellectual, must themselves mislead. You cannot, in other words, make use of the intellect to prove that the intellect tells lies, without invalidating your proof. The facts of evolution, for example, reflecting upon which Bergson was led to formulate his philosophy, have themselves been discovered by the intellect. If the intellect is untrustworthy, we cannot know that evolution is true, and the chief basis of Bergson's philosophy disappears.

Bergson suggests another explanation of matter as due to an interruption of the vital force. Life is likened to a fountain continually thrusting upwards; matter is the spent drops which fall back. Thus matter is spoken of as the reverse movement of the flow of life. It is still life, but life flowing in a contrary direction. But there cannot be an interruption in the vital flow, unless there is something to interrupt; this something which interrupts must be other than the movement in which it causes an interruption. Thus the necessity in the universe for some element other than the stream of life is again apparent.

The necessity for a further principle.

In the opinion of the present writer this necessity for a 'something other' cannot be eliminated. Bergson's is but the latest of a long line of attempts to explain the universe as being, or as being the expression of, one fundamental all-embracing thing or principle. It is a very attractive conception, but it is unsupported by proof, mistakes assertion for argument, and offers us not an account of the universe that is, but a beautiful fairy tale of a universe that has been devised by the ingenious brains of its authors.

Theories of this type, which assert that reality is fundamentally one and that the appearance of many different things which it undoubtedly presents is illusory, are called monistic. They attempt, as Bergson does, to show in different ways that the phenomena of the familiar world, matter, space, time and the plurality of different things, are full of contradictions and cannot, therefore, belong to reality. In my view these attempts are unsuccessful and, although I cannot here defend the assumption,[1] I propose to assume that the monistic philosophers have failed to establish their case. I shall assume, that is to say, that the universe is or contains more than one kind of thing. Theories which assert the existence of more than one type of reality are called pluralistic—or dualistic, if they affirm that the universe contains or fundamentally *is* two things or principles—and I shall now consider what account of the facts of life and evolution can be offered on a dualistic basis. I shall assume, that is to say, that both life and matter are real, in the sense that neither can be derived from the other, and proceed to a consideration of those

[1] Readers who are interested in this question are referred to my *Matter, Life and Value* (O.U.P.), Chapter II for a detailed criticism of Monism.

evolutionary theories which endeavour to find accommodation for both of them within the confines of the universe.

III

THE INTERACTION OF LIFE AND MATTER

Alternative views.

The difficulty that besets a dualistic view of evolution, a view that is to say which endeavours to retain both life and matter as distinct principles, is that of envisaging the mode of their interaction. I referred to this difficulty in the second chapter,[1] described the theory of psychophysical parallelism eked out by divine intervention which sought to solve it, and showed how the materialist psychology, which denied any ultimate difference between mind and body arose in part from the obvious inadequacy of that solution. Let us consider the various possible alternatives. Either reality is exclusively material and composed of matter, or it is exclusively mental and composed of mind, or it is composed of neither mind nor matter, but of a sort of neutral stuff more fundamental than either, or it is or contains both mind and matter and perhaps other things as well. The first hypothesis, the hypothesis of Materialism, we are agreeing provisionally to reject. Matter is much too mysterious in these days to constitute a satisfactory basis for literally everything that exists. The second, the hypothesis of Idealism, is capable of far-reaching applications but pays little regard to brute facts. Modern physics, it is true, has seemed to many to suggest an idealist universe, but, in spite of Professor Wildon Carr, Bergson and others, it cannot be said that biology, the implications of which we are here considering, or, indeed, any of the other sciences, suggests anything of the sort. As a personal opinion I should say[2] that Idealism may conceivably be true, but that, if it

[1] See Chapter II, pp. 35, 36.
[2] See my *Philosophical Aspects of Modern Science* for an elaboration of this view.

is, science can afford no reasons for thinking it to be so.

Several writers, notably William James and Earl Russell, have advocated the third view, but its implications are obscure and the reasons advanced in support of it are too technical to be considered here.

Let us then consider the fourth hypothesis.

Difficulty of distinguishing the living from the non-living.

Life exists; the fact is obvious. Either, then, it was present in the particles of matter of which the earth is composed from the first, or it was smuggled into it, as it were, from outside at some period in the planet's history.

In favour of the first hypothesis is the fact that life is nowhere known to exist except in association with matter. It may also be the case that matter nowhere exists except in association with life. I say that it *may* be the case, because, although there is some reason to believe that it is in theory demonstrable, it is at present very far from being demonstrated.

Meanwhile emphasis is laid on the impossibility of drawing a satisfactory dividing line between living and non-living matter. Many criteria of the difference between them have at various times been suggested. There has been the attempt to distinguish between things which moved of their own volition and those which did not, between those which had the power to reproduce themselves and those which had not, between those which absorbed nourishment to build up fresh tissues and those which did not. Modern research has shown that none of these suggested criteria is satisfactory, and it seems likely enough that, so far as the material things of this planet are concerned, we may be driven to concede that there is no ultimate and final difference between matter which is living and matter which is dead.

Yet it is difficult to hold that life and matter are everywhere associated, unless we are prepared to accept either the materialist or the idealist hypothesis. For, unless we are to write off the invariable association of the two as a series of coincidences infinitely repeated, we are driven to think that there must be some necessary relation between them of the kind which is expressed by saying that matter is ultimate and generates life, or that life is ultimate and matter is the way in which non-material living units appear to mind. The former view is Materialism, the latter is Idealism, and it looks, therefore, as if we should be driven to accept one or other of these two alternatives. Nevertheless we are provisionally agreeing to try to retain both matter and life as separate and independent principles. How is this to be done in face of the difficulty just raised, the difficulty, namely, of the probably invariable association of life and matter, at least upon the earth? In the first place, it is important that we should realise that the fact that matter and life are invariably associated *on this planet* now, if it is a fact, does not mean that they always were; any more than the fact that all the matter of which this planet is composed is now impregnated with life, if it is a fact, entails that this is true of all matter everywhere.

Pervasion of Matter by Life.

Let us, then, assume for a moment that life is an independent, creative, immaterial force or principle, conceived after the model of Bergson's *élan vital*; that it is distinct from matter but is capable of entering into association with it. Let us suppose, further, that it is not with *all* matter that life can associate, but only with matter which, as a result of the operation of purely material forces, has reached a certain condition. To change the metaphor, it is not any kind of stuff that life can utilise for its purposes, but only a proportion of the material which the universe contains. Life, in fact, may, on this supposition, be likened to an electric current running down a metal wire. Some metals will not take the current at all and different kinds of metals will be capable of taking different potentials of it. Let us conceive, then, of life entering as an independent activity or principle into the make-up of this planet at a particular stage of its history, and proceeding to utilise the matter of which it is composed by animating it. On this view the fact, if it is a fact, that life may be everywhere associated with matter on the earth now, does not mean that life *is* matter, or even that it has evolved out of matter, any more than the fact that all the houses in a town are occupied means that the tenants have been evolved out of the bricks and mortar.

In favour of this hypothesis is the fact that this planet was at one time a mass of molten material, upon which the existence of life, as we know it, would have been impossible. It is only when certain rather rare material conditions supervene that life begins to appear. Even to-day life is possible only within a narrow layer or stratum of the universe, a few miles thick; it is to all intents and purposes tied to the surface of the earth; it cannot penetrate more than a mile or so below that surface nor exist more than a few miles above it.

This suggests that it is only matter which has reached a certain stage of development that life is able to utilise. And this stage may well be very rare. The point is of interest in connection with the researches upon which biochemists are engaged in connection with the production of protoplasm—that is to say, the material stuff of which living organisms are constructed. Many of the organic compounds found in living organisms, or secreted by them—such as urea, sugar, or starch—can already be manufactured in the laboratory. Hence, it is said that, if we could continue the manufacture of these organic compounds until we had made a mass of protoplasm, and could subject the protoplasm to suitable treatment, we might expect it to exhibit the phenomena of living organisms. As to the likelihood of this development I am not competent to express an opinion. It is important, however, to emphasise the fact that its realisation would in no sense be tantamount to the creation of life. What we have suggested is that the material universe, at first lifeless, in course of time reached a stage suitable for the reception of life. Now, there appears to be no reason why a stage of development which was once arrived at by natural means in the past should not be effected by human agency in the future. Yet, even so, it is not life that would be manufactured by chemists but only the material which is capable of receiving it. To identify the manufacture of synthetic protoplasm, which began to behave like a living creature, with the creation of life would be like saying that the builder who constructed a house had created the tenants who proceeded to occupy it.

Bearing of Physics on the Interaction Hypothesis.

What, however, of the difficulty of interaction to which I referred above? How, if life is immaterial and matter material, is the action of the one upon the other to be explained? A satisfactory answer to this question is not, in the present state of our knowledge, possible. Two points should, however, be borne in mind. First, the difficulty has been diminished by the modern conception of matter. It is not merely that matter has lost materiality and substance, that it dissolves into energy and is indistinguishable from the influences which it would be said to exert, if it existed; although all these considerations, by mitigating the hard solid 'lumpiness' of matter, facilitate the conception of interaction with the immaterial. More to the point is the fact that modern matter is so mysterious and elusive, we know so little either of its nature or its properties, that we can assert with no greater confidence what it cannot do, than we can assert what it can. Certainly we are not in a position to assert that it cannot be acted upon by influences which are non-material.

Views of Sir Oliver Lodge.

In this connection Sir Oliver Lodge, who is a prominent defender of the dualist hypothesis, has drawn attention to the anomalous position of the conception of force in the world of physics. The old notion of 'force' presupposed action at a distance; when the gravitational pull of the earth caused the apple to fall, the earth, it was obvious, was not actually touching the apple; it was thought, therefore, to be exerting influence upon the apple from a distance. The notion of influence or action from a distance has, however, been abandoned in modern physics, and the old conception of 'force' is, therefore, no longer held. Every particle, according to Einstein's general theory of relativity, moves along the line of least resistance. It moves, that is to say, along the easiest path open to it. It is true that it moves *as if* it were attracted by a distant body, but in fact it is the state of the gravitational field actually in contact with the particle at each moment of its course that guides it. Yet the properties of the gravitational field in question, in virtue of which the particle behaves in a certain way are invisible, and, but for the movement of the particle, would be unsuspected. Similarly, the deflection of the needle of a galvonometer, or the movements of a piece of iron in a magnetic field, will demonstrate electrical or magnetic properties in the space immediately in contact with them. It follows that when in the case of A and B, two non-contiguous objects, A appears to exert an influence upon B, we must infer that at every point of space between them something is happening which is specially associated with A. It is the occurrence of this something at the place in space where B is that produces the so-called effects of A upon B. Thus physics substitutes a series of continuously linked events in space for the old notion of force operating from a distance. It follows that every point of space must be supposed to be the theatre of an immense number of invisible happenings. The action of the sunlight affords a good example of this truth. 'All that we see in a wooded landscape is due to energy which has arrived through space, and represents a storage of that energy in visible and tangible form. The energy has, as it were, become incarnate in matter.'[1]

[1] Sir Oliver Lodge. 'On the Asserted difficulty of the Spiritualistic Hypothesis from the Scientific Point of View.' Proceedings of the Psychical Research Society. Part III, Vol. 38, pp. 491–493.

Sir Oliver Lodge argues that, if physics requires us to suppose that events in space which are not discernible by our senses or our instruments can not only occur but can influence material things, there is no inherent difficulty in supposing that psychical happenings can do the same. The motions which are observed in the affected piece of matter are not the same as those properties and events in space of which they are the index; they merely point to invisible events occurring outside themselves. Similarly, in Sir Oliver Lodge's view, 'The organism is the index or demonstrator of something beyond itself, something which, though it may be said to be incarnate in matter, has its more real and personal existence in some other region'.[1] Just as we infer the properties of an electric field from its effect on what we call charged bodies, and of a magnetic field from the behaviour of magnetised substances, so, Sir Oliver Lodge thinks, 'we might investigate the nature of an animating spirit from the behaviour of the organism on which we presume it acts'.[2]

Sir Oliver Lodge makes use of this argument in support of the hypothesis that spirit agencies can act upon inanimate objects and upon the material bodies of mediums. I do not wish to press this suggestion, which I shall briefly consider in a later chapter. It is sufficient for my purpose to emphasise the fact that modern physics appears to require the view that all material bodies are exposed at all moments to the influence of immense numbers of unseen non-material events which occur in space. The notion of a non-material form of life acting upon and using material bodies is, therefore, no longer so difficult to sustain as it was when the older physics held sway.

How is Interaction to be conceived?

In the second place, much depends upon the way in which interaction is conceived. I spoke in the first

[1-2] Sir Oliver Lodge. 'On the Asserted difficulty of the Spiritualistic Hypothesis from the Scientific Point of View.' Proceedings of the Psychical Research Society. Part III, Vol. 38, pp. 491–493.

chapter of the old-fashioned materialist conception of the mind which represented it metaphorically as the halo round the head of a saint. The conception still persists; Sir Arthur Keith, for example, frequently makes use of the analogy of the flame of the candle to indicate the status of the mind and its relation to the body. Just as the flame disappears when the candle is burnt out, so the mind disappears when the body breaks up. But this analogy begs the question, as can be seen at once if we substitute another one.

Let us think of the body after the model of a wireless set, and of life or mind as the wireless waves which it intercepts. Now, if the water in the batteries were exhausted, or the set were in some way damaged, it would cease to register the waves. But nobody would, therefore, be justified in arguing that the waves which it intercepted before, but intercept no longer, no longer existed. Similarly the fact that the body at death ceases to exhibit the phenomena of life is not in itself a reason for supposing that the current of life which it intercepted before, but intercepts no longer, has ceased to flow. All that we should be justified in inferring would be that the trap which the body formerly constituted for catching and canalising a current of life was no longer functioning.

If these metaphors are anywhere near the truth, life may be conceived to be intimately associated with but independent of the body. It is an activity rather than a thing, which uses and moulds the body for its purposes, playing upon it as the fingers of a skilled pianist play upon his instrument. Thus, it will produce effects in the body which are not due to physical causes, and which the body, if it were inanimate, would not exhibit. The body is a machine, and, if it is appropriately stimulated, will work as a machine works; but it is also guided and acted upon or by a non-mechanical agency, as the machine which is the engine of a car is operated by its driver.

CHAPTER VI

VITALISM AND CREATIVE EVOLUTION

Introductory.

The theory of Creative Evolution is not a coherent systematic philosophy; it is a body of speculative doctrine which embraces a number of conceptions which are prevalent in modern thought, even when they are not associated in such a way as to form a definite and comprehensive creed. For the popularisation of these conceptions Bernard Shaw's plays, especially the *Back to Methuselah* Pentateuch and, in a lesser degree, the works of H. G. Wells are responsible. The theory of emergence in its modern form was first advanced by Professor Lloyd Morgan, and the conception of life as a continuously changing flux, is, as we have seen, due to Bergson. The view which I am going to summarise, however, while incorporating elements from all these writers, owes more, perhaps, to Samuel Butler, that highly original genius whose contribution to modern thought is even now insufficiently recognised, than to any other thinker.

Individuality as a means.

I propose to take up the thread of evolutionary theory from the standpoint of the conclusion suggested in the last chapter, that life is not an emanation from matter, but is an independent principle which enters into association with matter, the result of the combination being a living organism. What the precise relation between life and matter may be we cannot say, but the Biblical metaphor which represents God as breathing the breath of life into clay represents fairly accurately the conception which I wish to suggest. A living organism may thus be metaphorically regarded in the light of an instrument or tool formed and used by life for the further-ance of its instinctive purpose. It embodies a current of life temporarily insulated from the main stream by the matter with which it is associated. Individuality, which results from the insulation, is thus not an end in itself. It is a means to an end which transcends it. What that end may be we can only dimly guess; moreover, any guess that we may choose to make is almost certain to be wrong. But the time-honoured view that the purpose of evolution, the end for which the whole of creation travails, is the preparation of a certain number of individual souls conceived in the likeness of nineteenth-century adults for eternal happiness, is coming to be more or less generally abandoned. It is reasonably certain that our own species will be superseded, as have countless other species in the past, and any view which regards human individuality as ultimate is, therefore, almost certainly mistaken. Moreover, if life, as I have suggested, is a principle which is independent of matter, there is no reason to suppose that its association with matter must necessarily always persist. If it does not, then we should be justified in regarding individuality, which results from the association, not as ultimate, but as a temporary device by which life seeks to facilitate its own develop-ment.

The doctrine of Emergence.

Inevitably, the concept of creative evolution stresses the creativity of life. In modern biological thought life's creativity is often expressed in the form of the doctrine of emergence. This doctrine, which was originally pro-pounded by Professor Lloyd Morgan, to describe the mode of development of living organisms, takes a number of different forms; it may, however, be stated roughly as follows.

Let us suppose that we combine the two elements, oxygen and hydrogen, in a certain proportion with the result that we produce water. Now, water exhibits certain characteristics, wetness, for example, which are not the characteristics either of hydrogen or oxygen; what is more, nobody who was acquainted merely with oxygen and hydrogen and had never experienced water could have deduced from the most careful inspection of these elements taken separately that the result of their combination would be water. In other words, some of the characteristics of water are new, in the sense that they are not present in and could not be deduced from an examination of either of its constituents. Of these characteristics of water we say that they are emergent, meaning by this that we cannot give a complete account of them in terms of the ingredients of which water is compounded. The human body, again, is composed of a number of different constituents such as brain and blood and nerves and flesh. But to take the requisite number of constituents of the right sort and collect them together is not to produce a human body, but merely a heap of flesh, nerves, bones, and so forth. For, in addition to the right quantities of the right constituents, the body manifests a particular form of plan of arrangement. When, that is to say, the constituents are arranged in a certain way, there 'emerges' a new entity which is something over and above the sum by addition of the constituent parts, and this new entity, the human body, is more than its parts, because it exhibits qualities which were not present in any of the parts, and which nobody who had seen only the component parts could have predicted as likely to result from their combination. A lung or a heart taken by itself is not alive, and a disembodied intelligence which had seen only lungs and hearts would not know what being alive meant. But bodies, which are hearts plus lungs plus other things, are alive, and this quality of livingness is an 'emergent' quality in bodies, just as the quality of wetness is an 'emergent' quality in water, because it is not present in any of the parts which are brought together to make the whole in which it appears.

The development of Novelty.

Let us now apply this concept to the development of life itself. When we say that the development of life proceeds by emergence, we mean that it consists in the continual throwing up of new qualities which were not present in any of the antecedents from which the entity possessing the qualities sprang. The evolution of living organisms is, indeed, nothing but the incessant appearance in the universe of new qualities, new powers, new activities, new modes of behaviour, new attributes of knowledge and skill of which there is no antecedent in the component parts, no manifest promise in the germ itself. Hence, the occurrence of variations in species, which, as we have seen, presents an insurmountable difficulty to the materialist view of evolution, is merely a particular and rather sensational example of a process which is going on all the time. Life, then, proceeds by the development of novelties; it is, by its very nature, that which is always bringing to birth what is new.

That some conception of this kind is entailed by the growth of living creatures seems on reflection to be forced upon us. The growth of a living creature palpably involves the continuous appearance of new qualities which were literally non-existent before they developed. Consider, for example, the quality of knowledge or understanding which a human being exhibits. An engineer, let us say, knows how to build a bridge; a mathematician understands the differential calculus. Either this knowledge and this understanding are new, in the sense that there was a time when no mind possessed them, or they are not. If they are not, then they existed in some form when the earth was populated by amoebas. But this seems absurd; to suppose that the knowledge of the differential calculus existed *in vacuo*, as it were, when our planet was lifeless, still more absurd. But if there was a time when this knowledge was not,

E

then it is really new, or to put the point more picturesquely, it has 'emerged' out of nothing.

Similarly with living matter. The matter of which a living body is composed, beginning as a microscopic speck of protoplasm, ends as a many-millioned colony of living cells. These cells are highly organised, and specialised for the performance of different functions. Some are marshalled to carry on the work of the nervous system; others to form the engines we call muscles; others, again, serve the comparatively lowly purpose of bone-levers. Instruments of incredible delicacy, the eye and the ear are evolved; yet the whole complex mechanism of a living human body is developed from a particle of living matter smaller than the finest pin-head. Now, either these complex cells and organs were present in the pin-head to begin with, or they were not. If they were not, then once again they have literally been created, for, in saying that there was a time when the living tissue of, say, a human eye, was not present in the universe, we are saying that this living tissue, when it appeared, came out of nothing.

On these lines the purely biological theory of emergence may be expanded into the philosophical doctrine of life's creativity. In the world of materialist physics there can never be more in the result than there was in the cause. There can, in other words, only be rearrangements of what is already given; and all change and apparent growth must be a rearrangement of already existing material. But with life, if the hypothesis of creative evolution is correct, this is not so. The mode of life's development is different from that of matter, in that life is continually bringing to birth what is new, so that at any given moment in the development of a living organism the organism is literally more than it was at any preceding moment. The process of evolution consists, therefore, in the emergence of ever higher levels of vital development; and by higher levels of vital development we shall mean, at the present stage of the argument, life possessed of greater powers and endowed with a capacity for greater variety and intensity of experience.

Life as purposive.

It is implied by what has been said that the development of life is purposive. Purpose implies a goal, and development a growing capacity to realise it. This does not mean that life is from the first imbued with a clear consciousness of its goal or, indeed, that anything of the nature of *conscious* purpose can initially be predicated of it. The life of the jelly fish and the amoeba is, it is obvious, not purposive in this sense. It is, indeed, only by courtesy that it can be called purposive at all. Life is conceived initially as a mere blind thrust or impulsion, a 'will to live' as Schopenhauer calls it, expressing itself in a never ending stream of impulses and desires. Thereafter the quality of purposiveness emerges as one of the qualities that life acquires in the process of its own evolution. Thus the only justification for the ascription of purposiveness to life in its earliest manifestations is that, since such life is obviously continuous with the highly conscious life that is manifested in ourselves, what is true of our developed life may be supposed to be in some sense true also of life at all stages of development, 'just as', to quote Schopenhauer, 'the first dim light of dawn must share the name of sunlight with the rays of full midday.' Just as higher levels of life emerge, so does the knowledge that they are higher, and that they are merely a stage in a process which will involve the emergence of levels that are higher yet. To say that life is purposive implies, then, first, that life at any given stage of development is conscious that it has reached that stage, and secondly, that a further stage is envisaged beyond.

We are, then, on this view required to think of life as a force or principle, at first unconscious or possessing only the latent germs of consciousness, seeking to realise through individuals not only higher powers and extended faculties, but a more conscious realisation of the use to which its powers and faculties may be put. The purpose, in short, grows clearer as the powers needed for its realisation grow greater.

Life's Method Experimental.

Moreover, the process of life's evolution is neither infallible nor inevitable but proceeds, as Shaw frequently points out, by the method of trial and error. Life, in other words, may make mistakes, and experience setbacks. If living organisms are the instruments which life contrives to further the process of its own development, we must recognise that they are, even the best of them, very imperfect instruments, and will, no doubt, be superseded by better ones as soon as life can contrive them. Instruments which are adapted to its purpose at one level of evolution may, like the mesozoic reptiles, be unfitted to carry it forward once that level is achieved. The path of evolution is littered with the débris of discarded experiments, and there is no reason to suppose that the human race, once it has served its purpose, will continue in perpetuity.

Nor does there seem to be any necessary reason why the process of evolution should reach its goal or even develop higher levels of life. It is implied in the assertion of life's freedom that it is free to fail as well as to succeed, and if—to envisage a possible example of failure—the heat of the sun should prove insufficient to support the conditions favourable to life's manifestation on the earth, before life has developed to the point at which it can dispense with the necessity of associating itself with matter, we should, I think, be justified in saying that life's experiment on this planet had failed. This failure would not, of course, preclude the possibility of other evolutionary experiments taking place and succeeding elsewhere.

Struggle and endeavour as the mode of Evolution.

It is to Schopenhauer that we primarily owe the conception of existence as being by its very nature a process of struggle and endeavour. Shaw and Butler regard struggle and endeavour as the means by which development is achieved, and represent effort at one level of emergence as preparing the way for a jump to a higher. Life, in other words, assimilates at each level the acquisitions which facilitate its emergence at the next. It is this necessity for struggle as a condition of development which suggests a possible answer to the question: 'Why should life objectify itself in matter at all?'

Any answer to this question must necessarily be the result of guesswork clothed in the language of metaphor. Several suggest themselves which are complementary rather than alternative. We may say that in a material universe life had to become incarnate in matter before it could develop, if only because matter was the medium in and with which it had to work. Or we may think of matter in the light of a barrier, a vast obstructive bulk of chaos and deadness, interposing between life and some non-material goal that lies beyond. Dimly sensing this goal and seeking what it senses, life finds matter barring its path. To pass beyond it, life must first pass through it. Accordingly it enters into matter, and, moulding the stuff of the physical world into the instruments best fitted to serve its purpose at each succeeding level of its progress, manifests itself in all the infinite variety of living organisms.

But, if matter is a barrier, opposing the progress of life and constraining its activities within a material mould, it is not for that reason to be regarded merely in the light of an impediment. For constriction and limitation may not be without a salutary effect on what is confined. To limit is to impel what is limited to overcome the limitation; to constrict is to stimulate the energies of what is constricted, forcing it to develop a readiness in contrivance and to achieve a concentration of purpose for which the incentive and ability would otherwise have been lacking. A river never flows so strongly as when, confined within the narrow banks of a gorge, it meets and overcomes the obstacles of a rocky bed.

It is suggested, then, that in opposing and constricting life matter performs, and performs of necessity, the function of a whetstone, compelling life to enlarge its powers and sharpen its faculties, in order to transcend the limitations that it imposes. Hence our lives are lives of endeavour and struggle, in which we are of necessity involved, in order that we may achieve the ends which we consciously or unconsciously desire. Biologists recognise this when they tell us of the struggle for existence; but there is no reason to suppose that effort and struggle cease when the purely physical needs, which they were first designed to satisfy, are automatically supplied. Although we no longer fight one another with tooth and claw for the available food supply, we still struggle over wages and prices; although our efforts are no longer confined exclusively to the physical plane, the urge of life still finds expression in the effort to create a business, to paint a picture, to master the forces of nature, or to solve the problem of the universe. Creatures who feel no need to make efforts are no longer serviceable to life, which, in consequence, feels no further need of them. It is for this reason that those of us who by some chance of birth or circumstance are removed from the immediate incentive to effort and struggle—aristocrats, for example, or lap-dogs—degenerate and ultimately die out. The phenomenon of racial decadence is probably explicable on these lines.

Now, it is precisely through struggle, which we have seen to be the inevitable accompaniment of life, that we evolve and advance. Birds grew wings because they strove to fly; our remote ancestors, who lost their tails and achieved a precarious eminence on two legs instead of proceeding naturally on four, were spurred by an unconscious desire to walk. This desire produced efforts involving an increased performance of certain bodily activities and a growing neglect of others, with the result that living organisms came gradually through countless generations to transform their bodies in the direction unconsciously desired. It was by the same process of effort and experiment that the human race developed and refined its mental powers, with the result that the mind of the civilised man to-day transcends that of the savage, just as the mind of the savage transcends that of the ape.

Inheritance of acquired characteristics.

The doctrine just suggested commits us, it is obvious, to the view that acquired characteristics can be inherited. The affirmation of the inheritance of acquired characteristics is, indeed, involved by any theory which regards evolution as a purposive and not as a purely haphazard process. Acquired characteristics, as opposed to those which are inherited, are characteristics which we do not possess either in actuality or potentially at birth, but add to ourselves as we go through life; the ability to ride a bicycle, for instance, to do a sum, or to play the piano is acquired. Now, if these characteristics perish with the generation that acquires them, if the gains of one generation cannot be handed on to the next, then it is clear that the notion of plan or purpose in evolution and of a cumulative progressive advance in fulfilment of that purpose must be given up. The new developments which life may achieve in the individuals of one generation will not be transmitted to the next and perpetuated for the permanent enrichment of life as a whole, but will be lost at the death of the individuals who exhibit them as though they had never been. Life, therefore, will resolve itself into a mere succession of generations exhibiting variations which are the result of chance, and making acquisitions which are won only to be lost; it is not an ordered advance in which each generation rises on the shoulders of its predecessors.

The battle that was fought in the nineteenth century

over the inheritance of acquired characteristics is one of the most celebrated in the history of controversy, and the issue is not settled yet. On the one side are a couple of men of genius, Samuel Butler and Shaw, and a few unorthodox biologists; on the other, most of the orthodox biologists and practically all the biological laboratory workers. The doctrine of inheritance has two main difficulties to meet; first, a particular theory of the nature of the germ cell, and secondly a lack of evidence.

Weismann's Germ-Cell Theory.

According to the theory in question in its nineteenth-century form, as advanced by Weismann, the material which goes to form the offspring proceeds not from the individual's body as a whole, but from a certain cell in the body known as the germ cell, and from this cell only. The important point about the germ cell, in Weismann's conception, was that it was screened from all the influences that might affect its temporary possessor; nothing that happened to the individual could possibly influence the germ cell. Thus, the individual in his relation to the germ cell may be likened to a postman charged with a precious missive which he must not open, but deliver intact to the person to whom it is addressed, that is to say, to his own offspring. Just as none of the adventures which the postman undergoes can alter the contents of the letter, so none of the modifications which occur in the parent can affect the germ cell which he transmits to his offspring.

It will be seen that this theory, if true in the form just stated, effectively precludes the inheritance of acquired characteristics. Modern genetical biology, however, no longer subscribes to the germ-cell theory in the form in which Weismann stated it. Indeed it has so transformed it, that the time-honoured distinction between characteristics which are inherited and those which are acquired is in a fair way to be superseded.

The machinery of inheritance.

Biologists seem now to be fairly generally agreed that the substances passed from parents to offspring, which constitute the individual's inheritance, are numbers of separate packets of diverse chemicals embedded in a less diversified mass of material. These packets of chemicals, the genes, are strung like beads along the line of the chromosomes: the chromosomes exist in pairs, so that for each packet on one chromosome there is a corresponding packet on another. When the organism becomes a parent, it distributes to its offspring one packet only from each of its pairs, the corresponding second packet of the pair being supplied by the other parent.

The genes, therefore, constitute the raw material of inheritance. Nor is this inheritance confined to bodily characteristics. There are gene combinations for bad temper and sadism just as there are for red hair and pink eyes, or in theory, there ought to be. But whether in any individual a particular combination will or will not become operative depends upon the environment, the environment being taken to include not only the external circumstances of the organism, but also the constitution of and conditions prevailing in the rest of the body. It is not true that because one inherits certain characteristics, one will exhibit them. What is true is that one inherits an immense number of potential 'innate' characteristics, but that which of them one will in fact display depends upon the environment in which one is placed. Hence, the characteristics that appear under training are as much inherited as those that appear at birth; the only difference is that the former set require the application of certain conditions over a period of time to 'bring them out'. The distinction between heredity and environment, between innate characteristics and acquired is, therefore, a false one. Strictly what one inherits are not characteristics at all, but certain material which, given certain conditions, will produce certain characteristics.

The scheme admittedly is so far a purely deterministic one. It is not deterministic in the sense that what the individual will become is preordained by the supply of genes which he gets from his parents; it is deterministic in the sense that what he will become is the result of a complex constituted by this initial supply and the environment in which he develops, for neither of which can he be considered responsible. In so far, therefore, as the theories described in this chapter base themselves upon the assumption of life's freedom and hold that mechanistic determinism cannot ultimately be sustained, the account of the machinery of inheritance just given cannot be invoked in their support.

Mechanist account not necessarily exhaustive.

I have briefly sketched the machinery of inheritance in order to show that the rigid distinction between acquired and inherited characteristics can no longer be maintained. If acquired characteristics cannot be transmitted, then, it would seem, no characteristics can be transmitted, since we are quite unable to say which are acquired and which are not. But, if we are taking seriously the assumptions upon which this chapter is based, we cannot allow the implied challenge which the above account of the machinery of inheritance, if taken as exhaustive, offers to creativity and freedom to pass without comment. Hence, it is pertinent to point out that the view that the individual's initial stock in trade is *exhausted* by the chemical constituents of the genes, that he is, in fact, initially *merely* packets of chemicals begs the whole question at issue between materialism and its opponents.

That the genes in the germ cell of a great musician are different from those in the cell of his idiot brother is not denied; what remains to be proved is that this exhausts the difference between them. May it not be the fact that the difference of composition in the genes is the expression of some more ultimate difference, which can only be described in psychical terms? No biologist has ever yet attempted to describe the nature of the chemical change in the germ cell which has given the world a new religion, a great symphony, or a moral advance, and there is absolutely no reason to suppose that the activity entailed by such achievements can be accounted for exclusively in terms of an alteration in germinal material. That all gene changes mean changes in the individual is true; but that all changes in the individual can be adequately described in terms of gene changes, and consequent alterations in reaction to environment, remains to be proved.

Genetics not Relevant to the Controversy.

The fact is that the modern science of genetics, and the detailed knowledge which it has given us of the mechanism of inheritance, do not have any direct bearing upon the materialist-vitalist controversy. What the materialist must do, if he is to establish his case, is in the last resort what Weismann did, that is to refer back all differences of mental and spiritual characteristics to differences of germinal stuff. That nobody expects to be able to locate the origin of the theory of Relativity in a chromosome is true; but the theory of Relativity must, if materialists are right, be, for all that, the result of interaction between inherited physical predisposition and environment, since, on the materialist view, there are no other factors which can be taken into account. Inherited physical predisposition will be analysable in terms of the distribution and composition of packets of chemicals, and will be, therefore, material: environment is also material; hence, unless we are to introduce some factor of a psychical order of which materialism refuses to take account, we shall in fact be constrained to explain the origin of religion and art, science and mathematics, in terms of the chemical composition of germ cells and environments.

In answer to this position the creative evolutionist

replies, as we replied in the last chapter, that living material is only the vehicle of something that informs and transcends it. This, he says, is true also of germinal material. Now this something is, on the theory we are considering, a dynamic, vital force which by definition is free and changing. The changes which occur in the germ cell may, therefore, be at least in part spontaneous; they may be, that is to say, changes which exploit and are not merely induced by their environment. They may be, moreover, purposive as well as spontaneous, in the sense that they are expressions of a principle which not only informs the germinal material but uses it as the expression of its own drive for development.

Butler's theory of Evolution.

The foregoing section expanded and modified in the light of modern genetics constitutes the sort of answer that Butler, to whom it is time to return, made to the arguments of Weismann in the course of a celebrated controversy.

The chief difficulty, apart from Weismann's cell theory, which the doctrine of the inheritance of acquired characteristics had to meet was the absence of evidence in its favour. If a white man lives in the tropics and acquires a skin burnt to the colour of coffee by the sun and his wife does the same, their children at birth will be as white as their parents were; if you cut off the tails of a pair of mice, their offspring will be born with tails of the normal length. Biologists tried it and were never tired of pointing triumphantly to the results of the experiment. Quite so, said Samuel Butler, but suppose you cut off the tails of mice continuously for a thousand generations! How do you know that a race of tailless mice might not emerge at the end of the process? Obviously a characteristic forcibly inflicted upon rather than acquired by one generation has no time to establish itself in the race history of the species, nor has the species any incentive to adopt it. But take a characteristic which over countless generations a species has acquired for itself, and acquired because it wanted to—take for example the knowledge which a chicken instinctively possesses that it must at a certain stage of its development peck its way out of the shell. Whence did it obtain this knowledge? Butler pointed out that the chicken not only knows that it must peck its way out of the shell, but that it must grow a little horny tip at the front of its face in order to perform the operation. How does it not only know these things, but know them so well that it does them without thinking about them? Instinct, you will say; but instinct, after all, is only inherited knowledge, the things we do instinctively without conscious thought and effort being the things which our remote ancestors had to learn to do and to practise hard and often before they could do them with even tolerable certainty. The skill and knowledge acquired as the result of this practice constitute characteristics which are transmitted to future generations as instincts.

Instinct as Unconscious Memory.

Thus instinct is unconscious memory, the things we do instinctively being the things that the race has done so often in the past that we, remembering them unconsciously, do them without thinking about them in the present.

Originally, we may suppose, the species had consciously to attend to the performance of many operations, such as circulating its blood or growing its hair or nails, which we now perform instinctively. The transference to the unconscious or instinctive part of ourselves of processes which once required conscious effort and attention is an evolutionary gain, since it sets free our energy and attention for the acquisition of new powers. For example, we learn by effort and practice to ride the bicycle and to do the multiplication table. If we go on learning these things for a sufficient number of generations, we shall one day come to know how to do them instinctively, with the result that children will be born to our remote descendants with an instinctive capacity for balancing themselves on two wheels and an instinctive knowledge that seven times seven make forty-nine.

The example of the multiplication table affords, indeed, an actual case in point. It is only comparatively recently that man has been able to multiply at all. What every grocer does dozens of times a day was impossible in the Middle Ages except for experts. What is true of the multiplication table in general is true of all those mental operations which we know as 'doing arithmetic'.

'Computations which a child can now perform required then the services of a specialist; and what is now only a matter of a few minutes meant in the twelfth century days of elaborate work.'[1]

No doubt the increased ease of arithmetic was due in part to the adoption of Arabic numerals, with the consequent allocation of a place to zero; but it was at least as much due to new forms and habits of thinking among the peoples of Western Europe. The human mind in fact has literally made a new acquisition; it has acquired the power to think in the way arithmetic requires. Moreover, the adoption of Arabic numerals cannot be regarded merely as the introduction of a mechanical device, but, since it implied the power to manipulate them, must be taken to presuppose a general mental advance on the part of the arithmeticians who used them.

Butler held that cases of this kind suggest a formula for progress in evolution, according to which each generation knows and does instinctively more of the things which previous generations had to expend attention and energy in knowing and doing. Thus for each generation there is available a greater fund of energy and attention for the acquisition of new vital powers and faculties, which in their turn will form part of the inherited equipment of future generations. Vital progress

[1] T. Dantzig. *Number, the Language of Science*, p. 27, quoted in Delisle Burn's *Modern Civilization on Trial*, p. 257.

thus consists in the transference of the conscious acquisitions of one generation to the unconscious natural
endowment of the next, so that what is first acquired as
a faculty ends in being inherited as an instinct. In this
sense, then, acquired characteristics can be transmitted,
the machinery of transference being that faculty of
unconscious memory which we call instinct.

A theory of evolutionary progress.

We are now in a position to outline the general theory
of evolutionary progress to which the formula I have
taken from Butler points. The assumption upon which
we are proceeding is that life is a dynamic and spontaneous activity, which embodies itself in matter to form
living individuals. But, although it expresses itself in
individuals, life is not exhausted by its individual expressions; it transcends while it informs them, like an
exhaustless reservoir which is always more than the
individual currents which flow from it. From this
reservoir, according to the view we are considering, the
individual currents of life derive; to it they also return.
And here we come to a new point.

Just as the modern theory of physics envisages a
common source of radio-active energy from which each
atom of energy emanates, and to which, conceivably, it
returns, so, it is suggested, each unit of vital energy,
which, when associated with matter, we call a living
organism, reverts at the break-up of the body to a main
stream or reservoir of life, enriched by the skill and
knowledge, the more intense consciousness and the enlarged power of understanding which the individual has
acquired throughout a lifetime of effort and struggle,
and with these enriches in its turn the life stream from
which it took its rise. If living organisms are to be regarded as life's contrivances for facilitating the process
of its own evolution, it is clear that their struggles
and their victories, their acquisitions of skill and of
knowledge, the sharpening of their faculties and the

heightening of their powers—all the changes, in short, that happen to them in their lives—are not matters of indifference to life as a whole, but have a direct bearing upon its present status and future prospects. And the conclusion which this view of creative evolution suggests is that life as a whole is constantly being fertilised and developed by the acquisitions of knowledge, skill, and insight which its individual units make for it, and appears in consequence in each successive objectification of itself in matter at a slightly higher level. It is suggested, that is to say, not so much that I am the richer in vital endowment because of the efforts of my particular ancestors, though this may in some measure be true, but rather that the generation to which I belong enjoys life as a whole at a higher level and of a richer quality because of the acquisitions of all the preceding generations.

Philosophical significance of modern Biology.

I have summarised to the best of my ability and presented as a tolerably coherent theory a number of different speculations which have been suggested by modern biology. On the basis of these suggestions and speculations philosophical systems on an ambitious scale can be and have been erected. Those who are interested in following up this line of thought are referred to my *Matter, Life and Value*, in which one such system will be found. Of Bergson's philosophy I have already spoken. A system cast on different lines, which is, nevertheless, considerably influenced by the purposive trend of modern biological thought, is contained in Professor Alexander's famous work, *Space, Time and Deity*; another which derives chiefly from biology, is that to which General Smuts has given the name of *Holism*. Biological progress consists, he thinks, in the integration of more and more elements to form larger and larger organic wholes. The universe itself is, he believes, like a biological organism; it is, that is to say, a universe of whole making. To Professor Whitehead also we owe a profound but very difficult philosophy, which envisages the universe as an organic whole of which the living organism is an exemplar.

All these views of the universe, different as they undoubtedly are, have been suggested by the study of living as opposed to dead matter. They are founded, that is to say, upon biology rather than upon physics. This is not a book of philosophy, and I cannot therefore describe them. There is, however, one rather intriguing development of the line of thought followed in this chapter, which raises the whole question of the validity of spiritualism and the nature of the phenomena studied by psychical research. This development requires a separate chapter.

CHAPTER VII

ABNORMAL PSYCHICAL PHENOMENA: SUGGESTED EXPLANATIONS

I

RELEVANCE OF THESE PHENOMENA TO OUR VIEWS OF COSMOS AS A WHOLE

Introductory.

It seems appropriate at this point to give some account of the study of abnormal phenomena which has been pursued with considerable and increasing success since the war. By abnormal phenomena I mean those which are investigated by persons interested in psychical research, and which are frequently although erroneously supposed to prove the hypothesis known as spiritualism, and to establish the fact of human survival. I include an account of these phenomena and a brief summary of modern views on the subject at this point, because the hypothesis elaborated in the last chapter favours the supposition that some of them may be valid, in so far as it conceives of life, of mind, of matter and of the relations between them in a way which is at least compatible with their occurrence. In this respect it differs from most of the views of the nature of the universe which have been traditionally entertained, which make no provision for such phenomena, and are unable, therefore, to countenance the supposition that they are genuine.

If, for example, as materialism holds, the universe consists entirely of small particles of matter arranged in different ways, then the suggestion that spirit or mind may employ, direct or mould the activity of material substances, as for instance when a medium's body is supposed to be acted upon or controlled by the mind or spirit of another person, is untenable, while telepathy or the direct communication between minds, clairvoyance and the divination of future events, must be illusory. Yet such phenomena as ectoplasm and the movement of small objects without visible agency certainly *seem* to suggest that some mind is acting upon and altering the forms or position of pieces of matter.

If, on the other hand, we adopt the kind of hypothesis with regard to the nature of the universe which Christianity requires, the phenomena of spiritualism become unintelligible. That the universe may be the creation of an omnipotent, personal deity is conceivable; that the human spirit is immortal and survives the destruction of the body is also conceivable. Given these two premises, we may further suppose either that God permits us to know the fact of immortality, or for reasons of His own withholds the knowledge. But that He should allow it neither to be known nor not to be known, but to be suspected merely, the suspicion being founded upon equivocal phenomena occurring in the dim light and doubtful atmosphere of the séance room, is to me utterly inconceivable. The atmosphere of the laboratory is clear and obvious; it is an atmosphere favourable to the discovery of concrete fact. The atmosphere of the cathedral is equally known, and, at its best, equally respectworthy; it fosters faith, encourages contemplation and sharpens the vision of spiritual truth. But the séance room with its all too close affinity to the alchemy and witchcraft of the past, its longing for a sign and its crude appeal to the appetite for thrills and the love of the marvellous, is poles asunder from either of these, and it is, to say the least of it, unlikely that a benevolent creator should go out of his way to choose it as a medium for conveying to his creatures profound truths in regard to the nature and future of the human soul.

I infer that the ordinary religious conception of the universe is unfavourable to the spiritualist hypothesis, and it is not without interest to note that most religious organisations condemn the performances of the séance room with as much definiteness as in the twentieth century they permit themselves to condemn anything, the Catholics, as usual, providing an exception to the prevailing anaemia of religious conviction by downright denunciation of intercourse with what they do not hesitate to call evil spirits and even demons and devils. The view that the communications of the séance room proceed from devils who are sent to tempt us is, no doubt, possible, but is unlikely to commend itself to the ordinary twentieth-century mind, which is apt to forget, or, if it remembers, to belittle the important part which devils have played in human affairs in the past.

Relevance of Idealism to abnormal phenomena.

The climate of philosophical Idealism is also unfavourable to psychical phenomena. Many of these phenomena, such as telepathy, thought-reading and what are called spirit messages, involve the assumption of direct communication between minds. It may be as well here to emphasise the point that normal communication between minds is generally regarded as being indirect. I have, it is said, no direct knowledge of another person's mind; I only infer its existence from the behaviour of his body. If, for example, I hear his larynx articulating certain sounds which tell me that the next train for X leaves at midday, I infer that his mind has become aware of this fact as a result of reading the time table or by some other method, because I know that the production of similar sounds by my larynx would in my own case imply and proceed from a similar mental apprehension of the fact about the train. I infer, therefore, the existence of another person's mind by analogy from the behaviour of his body; so, at least, the orthodox argument runs. But the claim made in respect of certain abnormal or supernormal powers is that they involve *direct* communication between the minds of two people without any overt behaviour on the part of their bodies, that, in fact, A can know what B is thinking and feeling without using his eyes to observe what B does, or to read what he writes, or his ears to listen to what he says.

Now, if Idealism is correct in what it asserts, matter is not fundamental; it is, indeed, not real at all, and mind is the only reality. In this event all communication between minds would be direct, since there would be no bodies to intervene between them and to afford by their behaviour a basis for the inference to other minds. The distinction, therefore, between inferential and direct communication between minds would disappear, and there would be nothing abnormal in the apparently direct communication involved in telepathy, since in an Idealist universe all mental communication would be of this kind. In general, if manifestation in matter by non-material agencies is, as many believe it to be, at once the explanation and the distinguishing characteristic of most supernormal phenomena, it is clear that such manifestation could not occur in the absence of matter.

Dualism favourable to abnormal phenomena.

This consideration suggests the reason for the special suitability of the hypothesis outlined in the last chapter as a background for the phenomena studied by psychical research. The theory there suggested regards the phenomena constituted by the normal behaviour of living organisms as evidence of the manifestation in matter of a vital force or activity; a living organism is, indeed, on this view fundamentally a dualism; it witnesses to the activity of a non-material principle in the material medium which it animates. If such manifestation of living activity in matter is always going on, the phenomena studied by psychical research would afford only a particular and somewhat unusual case of what is a perfectly normal proceeding. If mind is always acting upon and producing movements in the body, it is not inconceivable that it should act upon and produce movement in a table or a tambourine; it might even be able to affect and to manifest itself in a body other than that with which it is usually associated.

For this reason the dualistic hypothesis considered in the last chapter affords a congenial atmosphere for the occurrence of abnormal phenomena whose types and classes I now proceed to catalogue.

II

CLASSES OF PHENOMENA

The author's own attitude.

Before I proceed to describe the various kinds of phenomena in question, I ought, perhaps, in view of the highly controversial nature of the subject, to indicate my own attitude in regard to them. I have had at different times a certain amount of first-hand experience of these phenomena. This experience has been due largely to the facilities afforded by the National Laboratory of Psychical Research,[1] a body which consists of persons who, subscribing to no definite beliefs or disbeliefs as to the causation of the phenomena they study, endeavour by experimental investigation to learn more of their nature and their causation. The Laboratory, in other words, consists neither of believers nor of unbelievers, but of those who wish to find out. It is in fact largely due to the work of this Laboratory, in which evidence is collected and sifted by the ordinary methods of scientific observation and experiment, that the whole subject of psychical research, hitherto an ambiguous territory in which quacks have happily hunted dupes, is in this country in a fair way to become a branch of science.

By the courtesy of the Director, Mr. Harry Price, I have had the advantage of sitting with a number of well-known mediums, and have witnessed at different times

[1] This became in 1934 the University of London Council for Psychical Investigation.

a considerable number of varied phenomena. I have come provisionally to three conclusions; these are negative and unsatisfactory in character, but I may as well give them here for what they are worth. First, it is not possible to ascribe all the manifestations which occur to quackery and trickery on the part of mediums assisted by dupery and credulity on the part of those who sit with them. The manifestations are, I think, too widespread to admit of this explanation, and there is a small but growing number of cases in which careful attention to and rigid control of the conditions in which phenomena have occurred have fairly conclusively ruled out the cheating hypothesis.

In this connection it may be pointed out here that most of the happenings in the séance room are of an exceedingly trivial and apparently non-significant character. Tambourines rattle, wastepaper baskets fly through the air, handkerchiefs tie themselves into knots, bells ring, cold breezes blow. It is this triviality that to my mind constitutes one of the strongest reasons for regarding some of the phenomena as genuine. It seems to me in the highest degree unlikely that a clever conjurer could not devise something more spectacular than such occurrences, or that an unscrupulous medium, designing to make money out of the anxiety of bereaved relatives to have news of those who have 'passed over', could not invent more detailed and convincing messages than those which actually pass muster in the séance room as communications from the departed.

I shall return to the significance of this apparent triviality of abnormal phenomena later; for the present, I point out merely that it affords some contributory evidence for their genuineness.

Secondly, I do not think that the phenomena can be wholly ascribed to manifestations of the unconscious self or selves of the medium or of the sitters, or of a collective unconscious brought temporarily into being by the fusion of the individual unconsciousnesses of sitters and medium or by emergence upon such fusion.[1]

Thirdly, I do not think that the spiritualist hypothesis, the hypothesis, namely, that the phenomena are the result of the interventions in human affairs of discarnate entities who are the surviving spirits of persons who, once alive, would now commonly be called dead, has been established. On the contrary, I think that it is most probably false. In general my view is that no satisfactory theory which covers *all* the phenomena has yet been advanced, nor in view of their great variety do I think it likely that a *single* satisfactory theory ever will. It is probable, I think, that different types of phenomena are caused in different ways, but, although we may be able to guess with some measure of confidence at the mode of causation of some of them, others remain at present totally inexplicable.

With this preliminary word of explanation I can now proceed to enumerate the main classes of phenomena and outline some of the theories which are current to-day as to their causation. For a more detailed account of abnormal phenomena I would refer the reader to the book *Rudi Schneider* by Harry Price, Director of the National Laboratory of Psychical Research, which contains an authoritative and scientific account of first-hand observations of a highly productive medium, and, as regards the more speculative side of the subject, to F. W. H. Myers's classic *Human Personality and its Survival of Bodily Death*.

Variety of phenomena.

The types of phenomena concerned are very various, and the fact that so many different kinds of happening are loosely classified together under some such general description as 'psychical', 'abnormal' or 'supernormal phenomena' is sufficient evidence, if evidence were needed, of the confusion which attends the whole subject, and of

[1] See Chapter VI, pp. 127–130, for an account of the sense in which 'emergence' is here used.

the unscientific manner in which it has hitherto been approached. A convenient though rough division of the phenomena may be made into psychical and physical, into those, in other words, which are thought to bear witness to the abnormal activities of some mind or minds and those which take the form of the unexplained movements of pieces of matter.

A. *Abnormal psychical phenomena.* (1) *Spirit Messages.*

The most important class of psychical phenomena is the class of messages which purport to come from the 'dead'. I have put the word 'dead' into inverted commas in acknowledgement of the claims made by spiritualists that the agencies responsible for sending the messages, the 'spirits' as they are called, are the personalities of men and women who once inhabited ordinary, material bodies on the earth.

The messages are obtained in many different ways, but the normal method is for a medium, who is in a trance, to speak them in what, it is frequently asserted, are recognised to be the voice and tones of the 'dead person', who is accordingly regarded as a 'spirit'. The messages so spoken are often addressed to a specific person usually present in the séance room, the inference being that the 'spirit' is aware of the presence of this person, and is taking advantage of the abnormal powers of the medium to communicate with him. Sometimes, however, the agency actually controlling and speaking through the medium is held not to be the 'spirit' of the communicating person, but a special class of 'spirit' known as a 'control', who is apparently possessed of certain special faculties and aptitudes, in virtue of which he is enabled to make use of the body of the medium to send messages, and who thus acts as an intermediary on the spirit side between communicating spirits and this world, as the medium on this side acts as an intermediary between living persons and the spirit world. On this view, then, a message sent from one world to the other must pass through two telephone exchanges, the medium on this side, the 'control' on the other.

The status and the nature of these 'controls' is unfortunately very obscure. Sir Oliver Lodge, who has investigated the subject in some detail, reports explanations given by 'controls' themselves, from which it appears that the 'control' may be either the unconscious self of the medium, a secondary personality of the 'spirit' projected by him for the special purpose of communicating with people still subject to earthly conditions, or a 'mask' or 'personification' of the 'spirit' which serves instead of him, while the 'spirit' himself is attending to other business,[1] or an automatic personality 'such as is produced automatically through hypnosis or nightmare or anaesthetics',[2] or a special class of intermediate creature which acts as a sort of liaison officer between this world and the next. The confusion which besets the subject, is, however, such that the mysterious 'spirit personalities' who are met with at séances, are at other times spoken of as if *they* were temporary emanations from the spirit artificially manufactured by a 'control' and *intervening between* the spirit's real personality and the medium's.

The obscurity surrounding the status of the 'control' is typical of that which invests the whole subject. Two obvious tests suggest themselves by reference to which the likelihood of the spiritualist hypothesis may be judged. First, do the messages convey information which could not conceivably have been accessible to any person other than the person who has 'passed over'? It may be admitted at once that proof that such information had in fact been conveyed would be very difficult to establish; it would be difficult, that is to say, to be quite sure in every case and in regard to each one of the persons concerned that he did not possess and could not have possessed either consciously or in the recesses of his unconscious the information which

---

[1] See Sir Oliver Lodge. *Conviction of Survival*, pp. 29–33 (published by Methuen).

[2] *ibid*, p. 36.

purported to come from the 'spirit'. Generally speaking, it is only when definite arrangements have been made by a living person to transmit such information preferably by cipher after his or her death in demonstration of his or her survival, that some of the conditions necessary for proof could be said to have been established.

Inadequacy of the Evidence.

In a number of cases convinced spiritualists, such as the late F. W. H. Myers and Dr. A. W. Verrall, are said to have made such arrangements while still alive, and in each instance surviving friends and relatives confidently report having entered into communication with the person in question after his death. But, so far as I am aware, the messages which have purported to come from the person who has 'passed over' have in no instance provided the desired proof by supplying information which could have been known only to the person who before death made the arrangement. In those cases in which proof of this nature has been asserted—and in many cases it has—it has not been found satisfactory by impartial persons who have investigated the evidence upon which it was based.

This brings me to the second question which may, I think, appropriately be raised when estimating the likelihood of the 'spirit' hypothesis, the question namely of the general nature of the communications received from 'spirits' purporting to describe the conditions under which they exist. These have two general characteristics; they are platitudinous and trivial, and almost invariably they reproduce the general culture, outlook and ideas of the medium and of those sitting with the medium. They are, in other words, such as persons possessing the economic, social and cultural background of the medium and the sitters might, if they set their imaginations to work, be supposed to have imagined, and they embody no material other than what might have been supplied by the imaginations of the living persons concerned.

The accounts of the 'Summerland', as it is called, where the spirits who have 'passed over' spend their time, are banal to a degree,[1] and, if persons whom we admire or to whom we are attached, are responsible for their form and substance, we can only regretfully conclude that the next world is a place in which the human spirit lamentably deteriorates in respect, at least, of its intellectual quality. One is driven to the conclusion that, even if ghosts have souls, they certainly have no brains.

Yet it may be that too much stress should not be laid upon the triviality of these messages. There is a striking passage in the work of the late F. W. H. Myers, in which he compares the explorers of the uncharted regions of psychical research to Columbus and his sailors, whose first introduction to America was the spectacle of the seaweed, floating timber, and other refuse of the Sargasso Sea. 'If,' he writes, 'our first clear facts about the Unseen World seem small and trivial, should that deter us from the quest? As well might Columbus have sailed home again, with America in the offing, on the ground that it was not worth while to discover a continent which manifested itself only by dead logs.'[2]

(2) *Telepathy, Clairvoyance, etc.*

Other supernormal phenomena falling into the psychological class are telepathy and clairvoyance.

Telepathy, or direct communication between the minds of persons who are not visibly present to each other, may, I think, fairly be regarded as an established fact. If it is, it may be reckoned a normal, although rarely exercised, human faculty; its investigation like that of hypnotism belongs to psychology proper, and it may be omitted from this brief survey.

Clairvoyance, the ability to be aware of scenes and

[1] See, for example, Sir Oliver Lodge's *Raymond* published in 1916. This book which achieved enormous popularity contains accounts of ghosts who 'smoke' cigars and 'drink' whiskies and sodas.

[2] Myers. *Human Personality*, Vol. II, p. 307.

events not visibly present and even in some instances to divine the future, stands on a different footing. Cases in which such powers are said to have been exercised, although so frequently reported as to have fallen more or less directly within the experience of most people, are, nevertheless, extremely difficult to substantiate, and should be accepted only after careful investigation.

If clairvoyance does in fact occur, it is probably to be regarded less as an abnormal human faculty than as an indication of what on other grounds we know to be the case, that there is something odd about time. Under the influence of the theory of relativity, considerable attention has in recent years been devoted to the problem of time. Cases are reported in increasing numbers in which people appear to have experience of the past, and Mr. J. W. Dunne has perfected a definite technique for experiencing the future.

Experience of the Future.

This technique is described in an important and highly intriguing work entitled *An Experiment with Time*.

Mr. Dunne noticed that some of his dreams came true. Many others have discovered the same fact, but a number of sensational circumstances attending the verification of some of his dreams led Mr. Dunne to devote special attention to the subject. He invented a method for recording his dreams immediately after they had been experienced, before, that is to say, his memory had faded or rationalisation had intervened to blur and distort, and after a number of careful experiments came to the conclusion that they contained elements drawn in varying degrees from his past and his future experience. He was even able, after a certain amount of practice, to distinguish those elements which referred to the future from those which were derived from the past.

The question then arose whether this power of Mr. Dunne's to experience his future was peculiar or abnormal. He accordingly induced a number of his friends to adopt his technique of dream-recording with results so closely approximating to his own, that he was forced to the conclusion that to live in one's dreams through an advance though confused version of one's future experience was a normal human attribute. Mr. Dunne then set himself to elaborate a theory of the nature of time in the light of which such experiences should be possible. The future, he pointed out, if we are able to experience it in dreams, must in some sense exist, but, as we travel through the time dimension our attention is normally turned in such a direction, that we are unable to get a view of it. We are, on this view, like men climbing backwards up a moving staircase, who can only see the steps up which they have come; but the steps ahead of them are nevertheless there, although they cannot be seen, and will in due course be reached. Mr. Dunne's theory of time, known as Serialism, is highly technical and cannot be understood without considerable mathematical equipment. It is mentioned here in illustration of the contention made above that many phenomena which have hitherto been regarded as pointing to the existence of supernatural faculties should perhaps more appropriately be regarded in the light of information obtained by normal although rarely used methods about the nature of time and space, information which is regarded as mysterious merely because we are unable to fit it into the structure of our existing knowledge. We are only beginning to realise the extent of our ignorance with regard to the nature of time, and the supposition of the present existence of the future, is, to say the least of it, less untenable than the view that crystal gazers, clairvoyants, and others can really give information about occurrences which have not occurred, are not occurring, may not occur, and do not in any sense, therefore, exist.

The Reincarnation Hypothesis.

No less well attested than the so-called wonders of clairvoyance have been the stories current in all ages of those who have apparently possessed the power of going back to the past. This power has usually been regarded as providing evidence for reincarnationist theories. In certain psychical states, it is said, we remember experiences which we lived through in previous lives. This supposition is, however, by no means necessitated. To any theory of reincarnation serious objections are immediately suggested by a consideration of the facts of the relationship between mind and body to which I drew attention in Chapter II.[1] The relationship, as I there pointed out, is obviously very close. An invalid, for example, has a different mentality from a healthy man, a hunchback from a straight man; character is bound up with the secretions of the ductless glands; an insufficiency of thyroid produces a half-wit and an excess of adrenalin a coward. Change a man's body and you change the man.

If a man's nature is largely determined by his body, it is bound up no less with his memories. My knowledge, such as it is, is largely a memory of the things I have learned; my outlook on life the effect of the things I have experienced. If I had not fallen out of the window at the age of five, I should not be afraid of heights now. As one gets older, memories become more important; very aged people live entirely in their memories; in fact *they are* their memories.

Again, a man is very largely the product of his environment. I, for example, am a child of the twentieth century, with the outlook, beliefs and attainments of my generation. Body, memories and environment—these go far to make a man what he is; his personality is, at least in part, their joint outcome.[2]

Now nobody who believes in reincarnation holds, so far as I know, that one inhabits the *same body* in different lives. Obviously not, since we know what happens to old bodies; they become worms. People do not normally have any memory of their past lives, so that their memories

[1] See pp. 34–36.
[2] Not entirely, if the argument in Chapter VI, pp. 148, 149 is valid.

in each life would be different; their environments also would be different. Given a different body, different memories and different environment, the difficulty is to see in what sense a man could be said to be the *same* person in different lives. If I may commit an Irishism, if it is really I who live through each one of a number of different lives, then I must be a different person each time.

The Queerness of Time.

A preferable explanation of these cases of apparent experience of the past may probably again be sought in the undoubted queerness of time. A particularly well attested instance has recently been described in detail in a book entitled *An Adventure*, which records the experience of two English ladies who, walking in 1901 in the grounds of the Trianon at Versailles, walked straight into the eighteenth century and incidentally saw Marie Antoinette. Although *An Adventure* originally appeared some twenty years ago, it was only when the book was republished in 1931[1] that the names of the two ladies were given for the first time. They were Miss Moberly and the late Miss Jourdain, who were successive Principals of St. Hugh's College, Oxford. These particulars only add weight to a narrative which already bore the unmistakable marks of good faith, and which, in the intervals, has been made even more remarkable by subsequent research leading to verification of numerous details.

The Narrative of Miss Moberly and Miss Jourdain.

Briefly the narrative is as follows: Miss Moberly and Miss Jourdain, visitors to Paris, interested neither in French history nor in the occult, were walking in the grounds of the Trianon one afternoon in August, 1901. They met and were addressed by persons wearing the costumes of 1789; some of these persons were visible to one lady, others to both. They saw woods which are no longer there, passed by a rustic bridge over a ravine down

[1] Publishers: Faber & Faber.

which ran a cascade which no longer exists; saw a man sitting by a garden kiosk which is not to be found; and were accosted by a footman who emerged from a door in the palace which, through the destruction of a staircase, has ceased for nearly a hundred years to afford any exit. At the time the ladies noticed nothing peculiar in their experiences beyond a strange feeling of depression. It was only subsequently, when some weeks later they discussed the events of that afternoon, that they became impressed by the oddness of what they had seen.

On a number of occasions the ladies returned to the scene and devoted themselves to investigating the mystery. They established the fact that the woods, the bridge, the ravine, the cascade, the kiosk no longer existed, and that the door could not be used. Buildings and grounds have, as might be supposed, undergone many changes since the days of Marie Antoinette, but careful investigation has in many cases established the fact that the scenes witnessed by the two ladies corresponded in minute particulars with the geography of 1789. The identity of some of the persons whom they met corresponds with that of historical personages and their dresses were in the fashion of the late eighteenth century.

As an illustration of this latter point, Miss Moberly, but not Miss Jourdain, saw a lady sitting on a terrace whose

'. . . light summer dress was arranged on her shoulders in handkerchief fashion, and there was a little line of either green or gold near the edge of the handkerchief, which showed me that it was *over*, not tucked into, her bodice, which was cut low.'

Further details are given. Subsequent research gave reason to suppose that the lady was Marie Antoinette herself.

Seven years later, pursuing their investigations, the ladies read the journal of Madame Eloffe (the Queen's modiste).

F

'She says that during the year 1789 the queen was extremely economical and had very few dresses made. Madame Eloffe repaired several light, washing, short skirts, and made in July and September two green silk bodices, besides many large white fichus.'

Details are then given from which it appears that one of these tallied very closely with the dress worn by the lady seen on the terrace. This is only one of a very considerable number of similar correspondences, or verifications, if it is preferred to call them that, on points of detail.

It remains to add that on two separate occasions Miss Jourdain, visiting the grounds alone, had similar experiences and again saw and conversed with eighteenth-century personages. On a third occasion she noticed that

'. . . the whole scene—sky, trees and buildings—gave a little shiver, like the movement of a curtain, or of scenery as at a theatre.'

In 1914 three persons, who had lived six years previously overlooking the park at Versailles, came to see Miss Jourdain and Miss Moberly and recounted similar experiences. Their experiences had, in fact, been so frequent that they had become accustomed to

'. . . the light and trees and walks being in an unnatural condition, so that at last the whole thing got on their nerves and they went away—thinking that they preferred to live in their own century and not in any other.'

While admitting that the hypothesis of the present existence of the past is beset with difficulties of a metaphysical character to which it seems at present impossible to assign any satisfactory solution, I think that it indicates the most fruitful basis for the investigation of these intriguing experiences.

B. *Abnormal physical phenomena.*

These are not less puzzling than the psychical, but they are more definite and in some ways easier to investigate. They are roughly of two kinds, effects believed to be produced by means of or through the agency of the medium's body and poltergeist phenomena.

Procedure at Séances.

Phenomena of the first type are those with which sitters at séances will be familiar. A circle is formed, hands and feet joined, the medium is bound and held and his hands and feet are controlled by members of the circle. The lights are turned down with the exception of a dim red glow, a gramophone is played and the sitters are requested to talk and sing (the 'spirit control' is said to like a noise), and in due course things begin to happen. They are trivial enough. The temperature of the room lowers, cold breezes are felt on the face and hands, flashes of light appear in different parts of the room, on one's lap, over one's shoulder, under one's nose. A carefully sealed cage contains various small articles rubbed with phosphorus to make them luminous; these are presently seen to move. Curtains sway and belly out into the room, tambourines and rattles play, a table moves across the floor, a waste-paper basket flies through the air. All the time the medium, still tightly held, is breathing hard in an apparently deep sleep. After a time the 'spirit control', who is supposed to be producing the phenomena, signifies by a prearranged signal, or sometimes by speaking through the medium, that no more can be done without tiring the medium. The medium is, accordingly, slowly wakened, the lights go up and the séance is at an end.

The above constitutes a very brief and necessarily incomplete account of the sort of events that may be expected to happen with a well-accredited and properly controlled medium, such as Rudi Schneider or Stella C. Sometimes the performance is varied by more sensational occurrences—for instance I have seen a handkerchief lift itself into the air, tear across and tie itself into knots—but as a rule the events follow more or less closely the course I have described.

If it is said that these phenomena are due to trickery performed under cover of the dim light and the noise of the gramophone and the conversation, I do not know how the assertion can be disproved. The issue is one upon which each person must judge for himself. I am completely inexpert in conjuring and belong to that numerous class of people who not only do not know how any of the illusions at Maskelyne's are produced, but have not even any theories as to how they might be produced; hence, my opinion on the matter is of little value. I may, however, register my conviction that the effects I have witnessed upon various occasions are not due to trickery and that some other explanation must therefore be found for them. The main ground for this conviction is the nature of the controls to which the medium, as the person chiefly suspect, has been subjected, and my personal knowledge of the other people who on various occasions have been present, some of whom, being conjurers, would be far more likely to detect any trickery that might be involved in the production of the phenomena than I should. To describe these controls or to enlarge further on the phenomena would be tedious.[1] It is sufficient to say that the great majority of the latter are of the same trivial and insignificant character as those to which I have briefly referred.

Ectoplasm.

What the correct explanation of these phenomena may be I do not know. The explanation usually suggested is that they are produced by means of ectoplasm. Ecto-

[1] Those interested will find a full account in the book *Rudi Schneider* (Methuen), by Harry Price, Secretary of the University of London Council for Psychical Investigation. See also *Leaves from a Psychist's Notebook* (Gollancz) and *Confessions of a Ghost Hunter* (Longmans), both by Harry Price.

plasm is supposed to be the stuff of the medium's body which is temporarily dematerialised into a kind of amorphous, pulpy mass capable of being moulded into different forms. I have myself seen what purported to be ectoplasm issuing as a shapeless, fluid substance of the colour and consistency of congealed porridge apparently from the medium's nose and ears and protruding itself into the room. I say 'what purported to be ectoplasm' because, on the two occasions on which I have witnessed it, the medium was not subject to the rigorous control which has obtained when the simple phenomena referred to above were produced. The official theory is that wisps, bands and even ropes of this ectoplasmic substance stretch from the medium's body into the séance room and are used by spirit agencies to move tables, rattle tambourines, lift inanimate objects and so forth. Whether this is so or not, I do not know. To turn on the light, and examine the alleged ectoplasm on the rare occasions on which it is visible, is not permitted on the ground that serious injury might be done to the medium, if the delicate stuff of his body were exposed to ordinary light in its disintegrated ectoplasmic state. In the absence of much more rigorous investigation than has yet been accorded to it, I should hesitate to accept the ectoplasm theory. I do not wish to rule it out; I merely assert that it is not proven.[1]

The 'Margery' phenomena.

Mention should perhaps be made at this point of the most remarkable series of phenomena which have been reported in recent years, those, namely, associated with the mediumship of Mrs. (Margery) Crandon in Boston, since they are currently believed to have been effected by the agency of ectoplasm.

[1] Good grounds were later adduced for supposing that one of the most celebrated producers of ectoplasm, Mrs. V. H. Duncan, was fraudulent. Those interested should consult *Regurgitation and the Duncan Mediumship* by Harry Price, published at 5s. by The National Laboratory of Psychical Research (now the University of London Council for Psychical Investigation).

The 'Margery' phenomena are attributed to the agency of a spirit, that of Walter, Mrs. Crandon's brother, who was killed in an accident some years ago. If the accounts which are given of these phenomena can be taken at their face value, they have the strongest bearing upon the question of survival after death, so strong indeed, as apparently to establish the fact of survival. To mention only one set of experiments, 'Walter' (the expression must be pardoned; it is practically impossible to avoid dropping into the question-begging language which is characteristic of the literature of the subject) has been in the habit of producing ectoplasmic thumbprints. A bowl of liquid wax is placed in the séance room, and Walter, using, presumably, the stuff of Margery's body reduced to an ectoplasmic condition, has frequently made thumbprints on the wax. These thumbprints, it is asserted, have been carefully investigated on more than one occasion by a fingerprint expert, who has testified to the fact that they were not the thumbprints of any person in the room. It is said to be impossible to fake a thumbprint at short notice, and, as the wax is asserted to have been inspected and found to be unmarked at the beginning of the séance, the inference suggested is that some immaterial agency used the material stuff of the medium's body to make thumbprints of its own. The making of thumbprints and fingerprints by 'spirit controls' is, indeed, a fairly common phenomenon of the séance room, although I have never witnessed it myself. It is clear, however, that if the Walter thumbprints can be established as valid, they constitute an important and a very puzzling addition to the list of phenomena which we are unable to explain.

To the Walter-Margery story there is a sequel which, if it could be accepted at its face value, would leave no doubt of the *sort* of explanation which we ought to be prepared to admit.

It is said that certain small objects belonging to Walter in his lifetime, in particular the razor which he used on the morning of his death, have been carefully preserved and still bear upon them the traces of his fingerprints. These traces have been revived by technical methods and have been found to be identical in every respect with the marks left on the wax in the séance room. Not having personally investigated the evidence, I do not feel myself in a position to comment upon this story. Its implications are clearly staggering, pointing as they do in the strongest possible way to individual survival after death. For this very reason, and not because I wish to throw suspicion on the *bona fides* of those concerned, it should be accepted only with the greatest possible reserve.[1]

Poltergeist phenomena.

Poltergeist phenomena are those traditionally attributed to the agency of 'earth spirits' or 'elementals'. They consist of the movement of small objects without visible cause. Observers have believed themselves to have detected an intention in the movements of these objects, an intention sometimes to divert, more often to mock, to humiliate, or to annoy, and have attributed poltergeist manifestations to the agency of elementary and somewhat malicious intelligences whose chief attribute is a love of mischief. The typical situation in which poltergeist phenomena are reported occurs when the earth is disturbed by the laying of the foundations of a new house. There follows an outbreak of trivial annoying acts in the immediate neighbourhood; doors and cupboards are

[1] Those who are interested will find an account of the 'Margery' mediumship and the so-called 'Walter' phenomena in *The British Journal of Psychical Research*, Vol. I, Nos. 5, 7, 9 and 10, published by The National Laboratory of Psychical Research. Bulletin III, published by the Laboratory in October 1932, consists of a paper written by E. E. Dudley, containing what appears to be convincing evidence in favour of the view that the fingerprints are those of a living person. Mr. Dudley's charges—for his demonstrations amount to nothing less—have been answered in a lengthy paper by K. Brackedd Thoroughgood, entitled *The 'Walter' Hands*, published in the Proceedings of the American Society for Psychical Research (Vol. XXII, 1933). I am not competent to offer an opinion on this controversy, but most of those with whom I am acquainted, who have gone carefully into the evidence, appear to regard Mr. Thoroughgood's paper as an inadequate reply to Mr. Dudley's charges.

rapped, furniture is moved, water jugs are overturned, bells are rung, children's hair is invisibly pulled. With these may be classed the typical phenomena of the haunted house. These manifestations often seem to be associated with a particular person, usually a person of less than normal intelligence, a half-wit, a child, or even a half-witted child. When the person in question is removed, the manifestations stop.

Owing to the fact that these occurrences, which usually take place in remote country districts, have a way of drying up when investigated by persons of competent scientific qualifications, we have to rely for our accounts of them upon uneducated persons who are both un-trained observers and inaccurate narrators. Some years ago, however, an opportunity occurred of witnessing poltergeist phenomena under controlled conditions, in connection with a Roumanian peasant girl, Eleanore Zugun, who was brought to London by her patron, the Countess Wassilko, and referred to the National Labor-atory of Psychical Research for investigation. The phe-nomena associated with Eleanore were of two kinds; weals or teeth marks would suddenly appear on her arms, legs or face without visible cause—Eleanore herself would attribute them to the agency of the devil—and small objects in her neighbourhood would be displaced without visible agency. Eleanore, who, although fourteen years old at the time, had the mentality of a child of eight or nine, would sit in normal surroundings and in full daylight playing with her toys in the presence of observers, when the following phenomena were witnessed. Small metal letters and coins placed on a ledge running round the walls of the room an inch or so below the ceiling would come tumbling to the floor; marked coins, which had been placed in drawers, would turn up in people's pockets; metal letters would invisibly transfer themselves from one end of the room to the other. On the arms of Eleanore herself marks, such as might have been made by teeth, would suddenly appear, and she would cry out with pain as she proclaimed a new attack by the devil. What the explanation of these occurrences may be, I cannot say. They are sufficiently well attested, but I am by no means certain that, in regard to those which I have personally observed, the hypothesis of trickery could be ruled out, although I personally do not feel inclined to accept it. Reports were in fact received later that Eleanore had been caught cheating, that is to say causing phenomena to happen by normal although surreptitious means; but the devices she employed were so childish and so easily detected, that they could at no time have deceived the skilled observers who saw her in London, and it seems probable that the cheating could be ascribed to a very natural attempt on Eleanore's part to continue to attract a waning attention by faking phenomena which no longer occurred spontaneously.

III

SUGGESTED EXPLANATIONS

Absence of any satisfactory theory.

I am conscious how unsatisfactory the above brief summary must appear. It has involved the description of phenomena for whose authenticity I am unable personally to vouch and, assuming these phenomena to be valid, I have admitted that there is no satisfactory explanation of their occurrence. And this is, in fact, the case. The investigation of supernormal phenomena is in its infancy; men of science still tend to fight shy of the subject and it has yet to emancipate itself from the atmosphere of credulity and superstition from which it took its rise. Supernormal phenomena have occurred throughout the whole recorded history of mankind. In the past they have been associated with witchcraft, astrology, demoniacal possession and the belief in ghosts and apparitions. To liquidate this legacy from a credulous past, and to disentangle from the mass of dubious and misreported occurrences the phenomena which deserve scientific investigation, is a formidable task, and it is far from being complete. Not only are we unable to say with certainty which occurrences are genuine and which are not, but assuming that some at least are genuine, we are unable to offer any satisfactory theory to account for them.

There is, that is to say, no single theory which covers all classes of phenomena, and it is doubtful whether there is any acceptable theory even of those falling within a single class. To the spiritualist hypothesis, which is that most commonly invoked, I have already referred. It suffers from the disadvantage of bearing the obvious marks of a rationalisation of human hopes and wishes. Most of us want to think that loved persons who are dead still survive, and some of us wish to survive ourselves; but this very circumstance should make us scrutinise very carefully any hypothesis which assures us that matters are arranged as we would wish them to be, and demand very convincing evidence before we permit ourselves to believe it. Looked at from this point of view, it is very doubtful whether the spiritualist hypothesis can produce any evidence in its favour which will stand the test of impartial investigation. At present it belongs to the realm of pure hypothesis.

Three other theories which purport to give an account, however partial, of some at least of the phenomena under consideration deserve mention.

(1) *The postulation of higher intelligences.*

First, there is the view suggested by the late F. W. H. Myers that abnormal phenomena may be regarded as manifestations of intelligences different from and probably higher than our own. Misrepresentation of writers' opinions on this highly controversial subject is frequent, and I am anxious not to attribute to Myers a view which he did not hold. I cannot, therefore, do better than quote a passage from a memorial discourse on Myers delivered by Sir Oliver Lodge in 1930, in which his view is briefly stated.

Sir Oliver Lodge is speaking of certain strange occurrences in the séance room, including the formation of ectoplasm, witnessed by Professor Charles Richet, Myers and himself:

'Myers did not,' he says, 'seem so much perturbed by these strange occurrences, repugnant though they then were to the common sense of the other members of the triumvirate—a physicist and a physiologist; they seemed to fit into some enlarged system of philosophy which he had evolved as to the probable nature and comprehensiveness of the unseen or spiritual world. He was prepared to admit a multitude of possibilities due to the activity of dwellers in some unexplored region or some unfamiliar aspect of the universe; not necessarily departed human beings at all, but intelligences who had developed by long experience a power of dealing with matter in unknown and unfamiliar ways, even to the extent sometimes of achieving what to a normal being with full use of the limbs would be impossible, such as dematerialisation. An ectoplasmic hand which he had strongly held and determined not to let go, had dematerialised in his grasp; and this had struck him more than the more normal kind of movements which I had witnessed, such as might be accomplished by liberated or by extra and temporary limbs—that is to say phenomena like hand-grasps, strong clutches, carrying things about, and so on, which would be quite feasible to any normal person who was free to move where he chose. His view evidently was that it would be a great mistake to imagine that humanity, whether discarnate or incarnate, exhausted the possibilities of conscious life in the universe; that we were beginning a study of the powers and possibilities open to other intelligences; that our business was to ascertain what could be done without preconceptions or ideas of impossibility based upon our own necessarily limited mundane experience on our particular planet. The universe, as he often said, must be infinite in an infinite number of ways; and it would be in the highest degree presumptuous for an explorer to deny or reject experience merely because it conflicted with the explorer's own small ideas of what was possible. To Myers we seemed to be at the beginning of an extensive line of enquiry, the opening of a new volume of research, which would occupy the enlightened attention of remote posterity, however futile and inexplicable our early attempts at demonstration were.'[1]

There is nothing intrinsically impossible in this view; it may quite conceivably be the true one. There is no reason to suppose that human beings are necessarily the highest form of life's manifestation, although they may be the highest on this planet. It is pertinent to recall the argument of Sir James Jeans to the effect that there are in all probability several thousand planets in the universe in which the conditions may be such as to favour life.[2] We cannot rule out, therefore, the hypothesis that on some one or other of these planets living creatures exist, who are trying experimentally in the face of immense difficulties to communicate with ourselves. The fact that we misunderstand the messages, or that they appear to us trivial and non-significant, is no more a proof to the contrary than a barnacle's misinterpretation of attempts on our part to communicate with it would show that we did not exist, or that such attempts were not being made.

(2) *The 'Psychic Factor' theory.*

A second suggestion which has a certain inherent plausibility has been put forward by Dr. C. D. Broad. In his book, *The Mind and its Place in Nature*, Dr. Broad examines various theories of the relation between the mind and the body.[3] After an exhaustive analysis he comes to the conclusion that one which he designates

---

[1] Sir Oliver Lodge. *Conviction of Survival*, pp. 14–16.
[2] See Chapter IV, p. 64.
[3] Broad. *The Mind and its Place in Nature*, Ch. XII, especially pp. 535–550.

'Emergent Materialism' has a slightly smaller degree of improbability than any of the others. According to this theory the mind emerges[1] upon a combination of two other factors, the body and what, for want of a better word, he designates the 'psychic factor'. The 'psychic factor' is not a mind, but an immaterial element conceived more or less after the likeness of the vital force or activity described in the last chapter, which combines with the body to form a mind. At death the combination is dissolved, but it does not therefore follow that the 'psychic factor' ceases to exist. It may survive the dissolution of the body for at any rate a limited period, and during this period it may retain and exercise its capacity for combining with a body to form a mind.

Let us now consider the condition of the medium at a séance. The medium is in a trance. The precise meaning which should be attached to this expression is doubtful. Modern psychology has devoted considerable attention to the investigation of trance conditions, but precisely what account should be given of them, or whether the same account should be given of all of them is far from clear. Let us, however, assume the dualistic hypothesis, according to which the human personality is a combination of two distinct elements, a body and a spirit which animates the body, and suppose that the trance state really involves what it appears to involve, namely that the medium's spirit has temporarily vacated his body, or is at least for the time being not in control of it. There is nothing inconceivable in this hypothesis; cases of dual personality, which suggest that the same body may be the seat of two different spirits which animate it successively, suggest also that an animating spirit may be temporarily withdrawn. We will assume, then, without considering all that is implied by the assumption, that the medium's body is left temporarily uninhabited by his spirit, or that the normal connection between his spirit and his body has at least been temporarily

[1] See Chapter VI, pp. 127–128, for an account of emergence.

suspended. It is with this temporarily unoccupied or un-controlled body of the medium that, according to Dr. Broad's theory, the surviving 'psychic factor' of the dead person temporarily combines, and upon the combination there emerges as before a mind. This mind is a new mind, since the factors upon which it emerges have not been previously associated. It is not the mind of the medium, since the 'psychic factor' is that of the dead person; it is not the mind of the dead person, since the body is that of the medium. Also it is a temporary mind, continuing to exist only for the duration of the séance, or until such time as the medium wakes from his trance and his own spirit returns to control its body, or continues its interrupted existence.

Puzzling character of 'Spirit Messages'.

The attractiveness of this theory consists in its ability to explain the peculiarly puzzling quality of many spirit communications, which is not so much that they are unintelligible and inaccurate, as that they are not completely unintelligible and completely inaccurate; or, to put the point in another way, that, being as accurate and intelligible as they are, they are not more so.

Messages frequently convey information, which so far as can be conjectured could not possibly have been within the medium's own knowledge. The messages seem, moreover, at times to emanate from a particular source which, both in regard to the nature of its communications and the information it appears to possess, certainly suggests the mind of a person known to have died. On the other hand, as has been pointed out above, the messages are rarely detailed or definite; in fact they are so little detailed and so little definite that it is always possible to doubt their origin and the personality of their sender. 'If,' the sitter cannot help thinking, 'it is really my friend who has passed over who is communicating, why does he not speak more exactly and in detail of his condition and experiences, refer to those private matters that were known only to me and to him, and send words of comfort and consolation which are not vague generalities but have a special message for me?' Moreover, as I have already noted, many of the messages seem to bear upon them traces of the medium's personality, and to convey the sort of knowledge and ideas which the medium might be expected to possess.

This double characteristic of appearing vaguely to relate yet relating neither clearly nor satisfactorily to the dead person, and of appearing to relate to, without in fact expressing, the personality of the medium, is accounted for by the 'psychic factor' theory. The reference to the dead person is explained by the circumstance that the 'psychic factor' concerned is that of the dead person; the absence of definiteness and 'personality' in the messages, by the fact that it is not with the mind of the dead person that contact is established, since this mind ceased to exist when the combination of 'psychic factor' and body was dissolved. The reminiscences of the medium's personality are due to the fact that the medium's body is one of the elements upon which the new temporary mind emerges; but these reminiscences are never conclusive for the reason that it is not the medium's mind with which contact is established and which is responsible for the messages. How long and in what form the 'psychic factor' survives, the author of the theory is not prepared to say. The existence of a 'psychic factor' is, of course, mere guesswork, and the theory is only put forward as a hypothesis. Whether the reader will be prepared to accept it or not depends upon the general background of psychological presuppositions with which he starts. To a Behaviourist, for example, it would be unacceptable; but a kind of view suggested in the last chapter might with certain small modifications incorporate it with little difficulty.

(3) *Life's control of matter.*

The vitalist view affords, indeed, in a general way what may be regarded as a third alternative explanation.

I have already commented upon the favourable background which a dualistic theory of life and matter and of the individual organism as the outcome of their interaction affords for the interpretation of psychical phenomena. Life, on this view, animates matter, utilising it and moulding it for the furtherance of its own purposes. An individual is a piece of matter animated by a current of life temporarily separated from the main stream. In outlining this theory I mentioned the view, which appears to be gaining ground among biologists, that the phenomena of reproduction and growth could not be explained on purely mechanist lines. I noted too how the growth of the human body from a speck of living matter no larger than a pin-head appears to postulate the presence of some creative force or agency which directs the process.

The growth of an embryo in its early stages affords a particularly striking example of this direction and organisation of matter by life.

The development of embryonic organs.

There are roughly two different stages in the development of a growing embryo. In the first, each part of the embryo appears to possess the power of developing into any organ at need; in the second, the embryonic tissues become specialised, and are capable of developing only in one particular way. During the first stage the embryo, which is still little more than a fertilised egg, behaves as a single whole, in the sense that any part of it, if it is tampered with, seems to be capable of any sort of adjustment and modification to the needs of the whole. Thus, if a newt's egg is divided into two by tying a fine hair round it, each part will reorganise itself into a complete whole and produce a normal animal. Each part, that is to say, is capable of producing a complete set of organs at need, so that what, if the division had not taken place, might have been a leg in fact becomes an eye. Driesch's experiments on the cells of an embryo in the blastula stage referred to in Chapter V afford further evidence of the same sort.[1]

The same principle governs the development of embryonic tissue in a grown animal. If, for example, a newt's tail is cut off, the cells restore what is necessary and produce another; but, if the bud growing out to replace the amputated part be grafted on to some other part of the body, say to the freshly cut stump of a leg, it will, *provided it is transferred early enough*, grow not into a tail but into a leg.

It seems difficult to explain this remarkable plasticity on the part of embryonic tissue in its early stages, except by postulating some regulative principle which moulds and forms living matter in the interests of a whole. Everything happens as if the living matter of an embryo in its earlier stages were impelled by a drive to reach a certain appointed form, so that, if it is interfered with, it is capable of adjusting itself in such a way as to achieve this form as though the interference had not taken place, undifferentiated cells becoming eyes, ears, legs, or arms according to the demands of the whole organism.

Abnormal phenomena as a special case of life's control.

Now this principle of regulation which is exemplified by the perfectly normal processes of growth may on occasion operate abnormally. If, as we are assuming, life is an active spontaneous force which moulds and utilises matter, may not the utilisation of the matter of the medium's body to produce ectoplasm, and to mould that ectoplasm into the recognisable shapes and forms of so-called spirit manifestations, be an abnormal example of the same process as that which, when it manifests itself as the moulding and growth of the embryo's body in the womb, we regard as normal? Is it, in any event, any more mysterious than the normal process? We may even, if we wish to carry the fancy further, think of stray currents and eddies of life drifting apart from the main

[1] See Chapter V, p. 105

stream, but not yet objectified in matter, taking temporary control of the matter of the medium's body to produce abnormal manifestations. They may, for example, be responsible for those movements of small objects which we call poltergeist phenomena. But the fancy must not be pursued.

In speaking of 'currents and eddies of life' I have, indeed, already trespassed too far into the realm of metaphor. Those who are interested in such speculations are, however, recommended to follow their further development in an extraordinarily interesting book, *From the Unconscious to the Conscious*, by Gustav Geley, late Director of the International Metapsychical Institute in Paris. (The book, by the way, contains some highly intriguing photographs of ectoplasm.)

Explanation of abnormal faculties.

The vitalist hypothesis may fruitfully be invoked in explanation of other types of abnormal phenomena, for example, of those apparently abnormal faculties which are commonly designated by such words as clairvoyance and lucidity. (They are known also by the general technical name of crypto-psychism, to imply that such powers, if they exist, are normally not available to or are hidden from consciousness.) The possessors of these powers describe a man's past, claim to foresee his future and, by a flash of intuitive insight, divine his hopes, his wishes and his fears. They can grasp people's motives, peer into their minds, diagnose the secret promptings of their hearts. Perhaps the most striking examples of abnormal cognitive powers are afforded by the knowledge of the future and the past, examples of which were given in the second section of this chapter.

M. Geley has suggested that these powers may be perfectly normal vital powers which are nevertheless usually withheld from life's individual expressions. The purpose of the individual's life, we have in the last chapter suggested, is to improve the vital inheritance with

which he is initially equipped by acquisitions of knowledge, skill and insight. These are not lost at death but
qualify and enrich the stream of life as a whole in which
the individual current is again merged. Life, then, we
must conceive as possessed, through this continuous enrichment by its continuously returning individual
streams, of a reservoir of insight, knowledge and power,
far transcending the faculties normally available to
those separate expressions of itself which are individual
minds.

If we accept this theory, we may even hold that these
powers are actually present, although latent, in the
individual's unconscious, through which he may be conceived to be more directly continuous with the main
stream of life than in consciousness. Thus the unconscious is the recipient and storehouse of the acquisitions
of skill and talent which are made by consciousness.
'Everything occurs,' as M. Geley puts it, 'as though the
multitudes of daily experiences had as their end an unin-
terrupted enrichment of our unconscious during the
whole of life.' But assuming that these powers do really
belong to life as a whole, assuming also that they reside
in the individual's unconscious, they are normally withheld from the conscious use of individuals. If he could
divine his future, remember all his past, know all the
thoughts and motives of his friends, the individual would
lack the incentive to effort and the need to struggle.
Now it is, as we have seen, through effort and struggle
that new vital acquisitions are made. Hence life deliberately limits itself in the individual, withholding from
him its full powers, in order that he may be driven by
the fact of limitation to acquire new powers for himself.

But, although this limitation is the normal condition
of the individual, exceptions may occur. To one and
another here and there access may be permitted to the
full hidden powers of his own being. Some may even
have found a way of access for themselves, and, by discipline and meditation, have learned to tap the sealed

store of their innate vital endowment. It is in this direction that we may look for an explanation of the powers of the yogi and the mystic, and the humbler faculties of the crystal gazer and the clairvoyant may be traced to the same source. Many, no doubt, will find this suggestion fanciful and far fetched, and I have no wish to lay stress upon what after all can be at best nothing more than a plausible guess.

Telepathy and Clairvoyance.

There are, however, two considerations which may be advanced in its favour, considerations, moreover, which are derived from incidents which have fallen either directly or by hearsay within the experience of many people, and which are, therefore, fairly generally credited. In the first place, it is noticeable that most reported cases of telepathic communication occur in times of great mental stress. The typical case is that in which an individual in imminent danger of death communicates telepathically with a loved person who is known to be anxious for his safety. The mother sitting at home receives a telepathic communication from her son in the trenches warning her of his danger, or sees what subsequently turns out to have been a true vision of him lying wounded or dead about the time at which the wound was received.

The other class of case is that of persons who in danger of death have at the last moment been rescued. There is a well-supported tradition in the case, for example, of persons who have been nearly drowned, that, as hope begins to be abandoned and the individual feels himself sinking, a moment of clairvoyance occurs in which the whole of his life passes before him in a flash. Remote and long-forgotten incidents are recalled with the greatest vividness and detail, and years of experiences are lived through in what is subsequently found to have been an instant of time.

Common to both these types of cases is the danger of

imminent death to the persons concerned. In other words, to translate into the language of the theory we are considering, the separated current of life which constitutes the individuality of the wounded soldier and the drowning man is about to revert to the main stream. Is it too fanciful to suggest that, since the function for which these individual organisms were constituted has now apparently been performed, the limitations which, it is suggested, have been imposed as an incentive to performance, are withdrawn? The individual, whose lease of life as an individual is about to be terminated, enters therefore into the enjoyment of some of those larger and more extended powers of life stored up in his unconscious, which we have conceived to be normally withheld from him. He sees his past in a flash, and has the power of direct communication with persons not present to him.

This suggestion, once again, is put forward as the merest guess, but it will serve to illustrate the way in which the theory of creative evolution outlined in the last chapter may be applied to problems of abnormal psychology.

CHAPTER VIII

PSYCHO-ANALYSIS AND ITS EFFECTS

Influence of Psycho-analysis.

Most modern people have a nodding acquaintance with the theories of Freud. They suffer from 'inferiority complexes', 'sublimate' their desires and are the victims of 'neuroses', while young men, anxious to evoke suitable responses from the young women they desire, exhort them to get rid of their 'repressions'. This popular employment of the terminology of psycho-analysis corresponds to and reflects the wide area of its influence.

Psycho-analysis has had a profound effect upon the intellectual climate of the age, more profound perhaps than any of the currents of modern thought whose course I have hitherto traced. This effect shows itself in a number of different ways, but it may, I think, in general be summed up under two labels, Determinism and Irrationalism.

I propose first, to sketch very briefly the picture of the human personality presented by the most prominent psycho-analytic theories; secondly, to indicate the implications of these theories; thirdly, to trace the effects oı these implications in contemporary thought.

I

SOME ACCOUNT OF PSYCHO-ANALYTIC DOCTRINES

Common to all psycho-analytic theories is the view that the greater part of the human mind is unconscious. The human personality is like an iceberg; only a small part appears above the level of consciousness, the remainder is below. This remainder, known as the unconscious mind, or more simply as 'the unconscious', is not only the larger but also the more important part. The part which appears in consciousness is usually held to have arrived in consciousness via the unconscious in which it originated, so that the unconscious may be said to determine the contents of the conscious. The conscious part of the human being is not, therefore, the part that matters, since its contents and its workings are the expression of forces deep down within ourselves, whose genesis normally escapes detection and whose workings evade control. To discover and explore these hidden trends of the unconscious is the main object of psycho-analysis.

So far most psycho-analysts would agree. Differences appear, however, in regard to the character of these unconscious forces, the extent to which they determine consciousness, and the proper technique for discovering and dealing with them. I propose briefly to outline two divergent accounts which have obtained wide currency, that of Freud and that of Adler.

Theories of Freud.

Freud's general view requires us to conceive of the self after the model of two families dwelling upon different floors of the same house. The family on the first floor, which is the abode of the conscious self, are respectable, orderly, law-abiding folk, whose object is to keep themselves to themselves, to stand well with their neighbours and to preserve unsullied from the world their reputation for respectability. The ground floor, the unconscious, is occupied by a much larger family of a disreputable character. Many of its members belonged at one time to the first-floor family, but were dismissed as being unfit for its society and like fallen angels sent to dwell in the dungeons below. They are primitive, passionate and intensely selfish. Their one preoccupation is the gratification of their desires, which are predominantly sexual, and, the more effectively to achieve this end, they endeavour to return to the first floor, where they hope to secure wider scope and more publicity.

This endeavour is regarded with consternation by the first-floor family, who, in their anxiety to keep themselves to themselves, have hired a sort of policeman and planted him on the staircase to guard the approach to the door. This policeman is called the censor. It is his business to prevent any of the unruly elements in the unconscious, of which the conscious self would feel ashamed, from obtaining access to the conscious. Sometimes he is successful in his attempt and the primitive unconscious desire is kept under. Sometimes, however, he is unable completely to bar the way, and the unconscious desire succeeds in making its way up and appearing in the conscious. In this latter event, however, the censor usually manages to purify the unconscious desire in the course of transit, so that, if an inhabitant of the ground floor does manage to elevate himself on to the first floor he has to submit, as it were, to a process of being cleaned up and made respectable *en route*. This process of purifying unconscious elements which subsequently appear in consciousness is known as 'sublimation'. Sublimation will entirely change the apparent character of a desire which has undergone the sublimating process, so that an unconscious desire to elope with your next-door neighbour's wife may appear in consciousness as a sudden aversion from pickled onions.

Unconscious desires which suffer from continuous repression by the censor, finding their natural channel of expression in the conscious obstructed, are turned back upon themselves, and, like a river which has been dammed, form a kind of swamp in the unconscious which is called a complex. This complex gives rise to hysteria, nervousness, and in extreme cases to obsessions and neuroses, and Freud's claim was that by the mere process of bringing the complex to light and so drawing off, as it were, the stagnant accumulations formed by repressed desires, he is able to cure the nervous troubles which are so common in modern society. Freud often writes as if all the contents of consciousness at any given moment consisted of more or less sublimated versions of elements in the unconscious. This applies not only to the emotional and passional elements of our nature, our desires, wishes, aversions and hopes, but also to our beliefs and thoughts. A man's tastes in art or beliefs about religion are on this view just as much determined by the trends of his unconscious self as his taste in female beauty or his beliefs about his own character.

Freud's Later Work.

Freud's later work is largely concerned to represent the more mature achievements of the human spirit as compensations which we have invented for those instinctual renunciations which the existence of society demands. They thus come to be regarded as the necessary conditions of society's functioning. Religion was treated in this way in *The Future of an Illusion*, being derived from our desire for a heavenly father and protector to take the place of the earthly one who, as we grow up, unaccountably fails us. The conclusion acceptable to many people to-day, in its bearing upon religion, is apt to be disconcerting when it is extended to embrace activities which we are accustomed to regard as rational —to science, for example, to ethics, or to art. Thus ethics, which we have been wont to think of as a product of reason, is, on this view, merely a barrier which man has invented to hold in check the instincts whose release would make society impossible. Conscience, in fact, is society's policeman implanted in the individual. Hence our beliefs about what is right and good are determined by the nature of the instincts which society feels to be most dangerous to it. For example, the ethical demand to respect our neighbour and treat him as a person possessing equal rights with ourselves is a precaution against our instinctive tendency to hate him. It is not a rational precept, as we fondly believe; it is imposed upon us by the necessity of thwarting our instincts. The importance of art is derived from man's need to create illusions to protect him against the unbearable recognition of things as they are. 'These illusions are derived from the life of phantasy. . . . At the head of these phantasy pleasures stands the enjoyment of works of art.' Art is thus 'a mild narcotic', 'a temporary refuge from the hardships of life'.[1]

As with ethics and with art, so with science; so too with intellectual activity in general. We indulge in intellectual activity as a compensation for thwarted instinctive activity. What is more, the views we hold on apparently abstract questions are determined by the nature of the particular instincts whose substitute gratification is being sought in the intellectual activity which leads to their formation. Our instinctive desires, in fact, determine what we think true just as much as they determine what we think right; and the reasoning activity, which proceeds to provide us with arguments for reaching the conclusions which our instincts have already performed, is a sublimation of the same instincts. To trace the origin of so-called rational activity in the instinctive needs which it satisfies is to demonstrate the forces which determine both its direction and its conclusions. This is the work which Freud sets out to accomplish in his book, *Civilisation and its Discontents*.

Adler's Psychology.

The same conclusion is reached in Adler's psychology, although by a different route. For Adler the key to human psychology is the desire to compensate for an unconscious feeling of inferiority. The individual comes into the world weak, insignificant and helpless; ridiculously ill equipped in the struggle against Nature, he is completely dependent upon his elders for warmth, food and shelter.

Moreover, they dominate him psychologically, impressing him with a sense of their superior powers, their

[1] Freud. *Civilisation and its Discontents*, p. 35.

knowledge of the world and their freedom to live as they please. For everything he must turn to them, and the dependence thereby engendered imbues him from his earliest years with a sense of personal inferiority. To compensate for this inferiority the child strives to impress himself upon his environment. He endeavours to assert himself, to become the centre of interest, to win the praises of his fellows. Seeking to impress his natural will upon his environment, he is surprised when his environment fails to respond, pained when it begins to resent. And, since he usually fails in his endeavours, he takes refuge in the unreal realm of his imagination, revenging himself in fancy upon the world that slights him by casting himself in glorious and imposing roles in which he lords it over those who have humiliated him. 'Sooner or later,' says Adler, in *Understanding Human Nature*, 'every child becomes conscious of his inability to cope singlehanded with the challenge of existence. This feeling of inferiority is the driving force, the starting point from which every childish striving originates. It determines . . . the very goal of his existence.'

Thus for the ordinary child the process of growing up into a social adult is a highly formidable affair. More than any other psychologist Adler has stressed the fundamental importance for the individual's future life of the early years of childhood. For the ways in which the child seeks compensation for his inferiority determine the nature of the goal which guides his activities throughout his whole adult life. In Adler's view, all our activities are teleologically determined; their explanation is, in other words, to be sought not, as in the physical world, in some cause which precedes them, but in the end which they are seeking to realise, just as it is the idea of himself as winning the race which determines the exertions of the runner.

Not only to each of our individual activities is there its appropriate goal, but there is also a life goal which represents our desire to compensate for inferiority by the acquisition of power and importance in the community. This goal, which varies from man to man according to the nature of the inferiorities for which it compensates, is formed in childhood. Never realised by any, by most never even consciously conceived, it nevertheless determines what Adler calls the behaviour pattern of our lives, constituting a sort of framework within which all our experiences must accommodate themselves.

It is a commonplace that one man will see in a given situation what another misses, that one will enjoy that which fills another with repulsion, that, in a word, one man's meat is another man's poison, and Adler sees the explanation of these differences in the necessity which we impose upon all our experience of conforming to our goal and furthering its achievement. If an experience, whether perception or emotion, refuses to fit into the framework, we just refuse to have it. This very attractive notion suggests that we have only the experiences that we want to have.

The Life Goal: Applications.

This is no place for criticism, but it may be remarked in passing that Adler's psychology at this point lays itself open to precisely the objections which I urged in Chapter V against Bergson's conception of the intellect.[1] If we really have the experiences, and only the experiences we desire, why do we choose to have the experience of teeth drilling? As with Bergson's philosophy, so with Adler's psychology, I conclude that it is only in Heaven that it is true.

To resume, while it is inevitable that we should set up for ourselves these compensating goals, it is possible for us within limits to determine their character. It is here that the Adlerian psychologist comes in. Too often the goal is envisaged merely in terms of power over the community; it is pursued by a process of challenging rather than of cooperating with society, and, in

[1] See pp. 115–117.

so far as the individual is successful in its pursuit, his success precludes the achievement of their goals by others. Where Freud has revealed the beast in man, Adler claims to have exposed the devil, and the devil is simply this dominating urge to power and self-assertion. The more inferiorities, the keener the urge, a circumstance which gives us the measure of the inferiority of such men as Napoleon or Mussolini!

It is the business of the psychologist so to modify the unconscious desires of the patient that the goal of power over the community is transformed into one of peace within the community. Psychological health consists, in other words, in being dominated by a goal which can be realised in cooperation with one's fellows. Society is mankind's compensation for the biological weakness of the species, and to be at peace within society should be the individual's compensation for the weakness of himself. It is not in concentration upon the self, still less in the indulgence of imaginative phantasies of world power and self-glorification, that true compensation consists, but in the absorption of the self in some outward interest, in devotion to an idea or in self-sacrifice for a cause. It is only by forgetting the nervous little clod of wants and ailments which is the self, by losing the self in something greater than the self, that happiness is to be found. Such at least seems to be the practical outcome of Adler's psychology.

But are not such exhortations beside the point? Are we, in fact, free to give heed to them? The attempt to answer this question brings us to the general implications of psycho-analytic theories. These may, as I suggested above, be summed up under two heads, Determinism and Irrationalism. These conclusions result from the attitude which psycho-analysis requires us to adopt in regard to the will and the reason respectively.

II

IMPLICATIONS OF PSYCHO-ANALYSIS
A. DETERMINISM

Freud, as I have pointed out, holds that the origin and explanation of all conscious events is to be found in the unconscious. Our conscious thoughts and desires are, therefore, the reflections more or less distorted and more or less sublimated of unconscious elements in our nature. We do not know what is going on in the unconscious; if we did, it would not be unconscious, but, in respect of our knowledge of it, conscious; therefore we cannot control it.

If we do not know it and cannot control it, we are not responsible for it; therefore, we are not responsible for the particular version of it that appears in consciousness. In other words, we are not responsible for our conscious thoughts and desires. Our thoughts determine what we think, our desires what we do; therefore, we are not responsible for what we think and do. If, in short, consciousness is regarded as a by-product of unconscious processes, it is clearly determined by the processes which produce it. Conscious events are merely the smoke and flame given off by the workings of the subterranean psychological machinery of which we are unconscious.

Freedom of the Will.

But at this point it may very naturally be objected that no account is being taken of the will. It is true, it may be said, that our desires and thoughts occur to a large extent without our volition; but whether we encourage them or not is a different matter; whether we indulge our thoughts and gratify our desires depends upon our will. It is the function of will to control thought and discipline desire, and in exercising this control will is free. The feeling that we ought not to do this

or that, implies, as Kant pointed out, that we can prevent ourselves from doing it, and, although of course
the will may not prove effective in preventing us from
doing what we ought not to do, it always, we feel, could
have been effective. Thus in using our wills to control
our desires, to choose this and to refrain from that, we are
really free agents. Similarly with our tastes; we cannot,
admittedly, guarantee that we shall like doing this or
doing that, but we can guarantee that we will do this or
that, whether we like it or not.

This traditional doctrine of the will which insists
upon its essential freedom, and in particular upon its
efficacy in suppressing unruly desires, is vividly expressed by a famous simile of Plato's. Plato likened our
various desires to a number of unruly horses harnessed
to a chariot. Each horse is anxious to pull the chariot in
the direction in which it itself wishes to go, and is indifferent to the wishes of the rest. If, therefore, each
horse is allowed to indulge its wishes unchecked, the
chariot will oscillate violently between one course and
another, and will very likely come to a dead stop.
Within the chariot, however, there sits a charioteer. It
is his business to control the horses, guiding and re-
straining them in such a way that, instead of dissipating
their energies by striving against each other, they will
pull harmoniously together and draw the chariot along
a consistent and prearranged course. With this object
he allows to each horse only so much indulgence as is
compatible with the necessity of keeping the chariot to
a straight course, and with the fulfilment of some part
of the wishes of the other horses. Translating this simile
into the language of human psychology, we may say
that, in addition to the various self-regarding desires,
there is a further and separate desire for what is called
the good of the whole. This desire for the good of the
whole may be compared to the charioteer, and its function is to dovetail the various, unruly, self-regarding
desires into a harmonious system, so that no one desire

obtains more satisfaction than is consistent with the good of the whole. The desire for the good of the whole may be termed the will.

It is exceedingly doubtful whether, if the view which psycho-analysis takes of the human personality is a true one, this traditional analysis can be sustained. Psycho-analysis suggests that the fundamental motive forces of our natures are instinctive and impulsive in character. Now the will is either one among such forces or is a sub-limated version of such a force. It is, that is to say, either an instinctive drive to act in a certain way, or, if it is not, it cannot be brought into operation unless there is an instinctive drive to use it in a certain way.

A Modern Theory of Instinct.

This attitude to the will is by no means confined to psycho-analysts. It is prevalent in the writings of many modern psychologists. Professor McDougall, for ex-ample, perhaps the best known of modern writers on psychology, holds that the primary motive forces of human nature are the instincts. We have instincts to behave in certain ways. We act, in short, to satisfy our instincts, and, without the prompting of an instinct seek-ing its satisfaction, we can neither act nor think.

'The instincts,' says Professor McDougall, 'are the prime movers of all human activity; by the conative or impulsive force of some instinct every train of thought, however cold and passionless it may seem, is borne along towards its end . . . all the complex intellectual apparatus of the most highly developed mind is but the instrument by which these impulses seek their satisfaction. . . . Take away these instinctive dispositions, with their powerful mechanisms, and the organism would become incapable of activity of any kind; it would be inert and motionless, like a wonderful piece of clockwork whose mainspring had been removed.'[1]

[1] McDougall, *Outline of Psychology*, p. 218.

On this view, then, the instincts play a part analogous to that of the unconscious in Freud's theory. Even if we admit that there is in our mental make-up a separate, independent something called the will, it remains inoperative unless the urge of instinct is brought into play to set it going. Unless, therefore, we desire to use the will to suppress an unruly desire, we cannot in fact suppress it. Now the desire to use the will for this purpose is, like our other desires, an event which is fundamentally instinctive in character, for the occurrence and strength of which we cannot be held to be responsible.

Bearing of the foregoing on Self-Control.

What happens is that we are aware at the same time of two different urges or promptings to action. The first takes the form of an unruly self-regarding desire; the second is a desire to suppress the unruly desire in the interests of the good of the whole. If the first desire is stronger than the second, there will be a failure in what we call will, and we shall be said in common parlance to 'give way to our desire'. If the second desire is stronger than the first, we shall perform what is called an act of self-denial. This act of self-denial however, just as truly as the contrary act of self-indulgence, will be an expression of obedience to whatever happens to be our strongest desire at the moment. Hence, whatever the resultant action may be, it must be interpreted as a result of a conflict between two instinctive desires, a conflict in which the stronger will inevitably win.

The truth of this analysis has been obscured by the use of ambiguous phrases such as self-control and self-denial. These phrases suggest that in controlling a desire I am in some unexplained way acting in defiance of my nature. But it is only by drawing upon my own *natural* forces that I can defy my nature. If it were not *natural* for me to restrain my desire, I could not restrain it, so that in self-denial and self-control I am being just as truly self-indulgent as in an indiscriminate yielding to purely self-regarding desires.

G

Summing up we may say that, if the view that the basis of all action is an impulse is correct, the use of the will to repress desire is only a sublimated version of a desire to suppress another desire which we consider to be inimical to the good of the whole. If we desire to pass an examination, we *will* to suppress a desire to go to the cinema when we ought to be studying. But the *will* in this case is nothing more nor less than the expression of the desire to pass the examination, for which we are no more responsible than for the desire to go to the cinema.

Function of Conscience.

A similar conclusion emerges in regard to conscience. If the will has been traditionally regarded as the faculty by means of which we restrain ourselves from the performance of actions which are known to be wrong, conscience is traditionally the faculty by means of which their wrongness is recognised. It is the function of conscience to tell us when a desire may be justifiably indulged and when it may not. Conscience in fact has been envisaged as a sort of barmaid of the soul. She countenances in the desires such indulgence as propriety permits. She countenances them, in other words, for a time and up to a point, and then: 'Time's up, gentlemen,' she says, 'no more drinking after 10.30', and closes the bar. If gentlemen continue to drink after the warning of conscience, they get into trouble with the law. In other words, conscience gives them a bad time; remorse follows, and steps are taken to ensure more seemly conduct in future. In virtue of its performance of this inhibitory function, conscience, which may be described as the faculty whereby we prescribe certain things to be right and certain things to be wrong, has been regarded as the keystone of morality.

But morality is a structure built on the twin pillars of praise and blame. If you cannot blame a man for doing wrong, and cannot give him credit for doing right, morality goes by the board. Yet praise and blame are equally illogical, where there is no responsibility for the actions which attract the one and provoke the other. If, therefore, the analysis described above does, as it appears to do, strike successfully at the basis of human responsibility, the feeling of shame at wrongdoing, which is the chief expression of conscience, is a feeling for which we are no more responsible than for the desire to do wrong. If the feeling of shame is stronger than the desire to do wrong, conscience will prove effective in inhibiting wrong action. If, however, it is weaker, we shall act wrongly. Once again there is a conflict in which the victory will go to the stronger. For neither feeling nor for the strength of either feeling can we be held responsible.

Effect upon Ethics.

In this way the implications of the new psychology cut away the basis from traditional Ethics. In so doing they have engendered a fatalistic attitude to human nature which affects conduct in two ways. On the one hand, we are no longer so apt to blame persons for acting in ways of which we disapprove, holding that the offender is the victim of a complex, or is impelled by forces in his nature which he is unable to control. *Tout comprendre* in fact is *tout pardonner*. On the other hand, people are no longer so concerned as they used to be to strive at all costs to do what they consider to be right; nor do they feel remorse, if they fail, since they believe that their efforts will in any event be only such as their nature permits them to make, and that they cannot by exercise of will intensify them. If it is in our nature to desire what we lack the will to achieve, that is our misfortune, but it can no more be helped than a love of music coupled with a bad ear, or a wish to excel at games in one who has a bad eye for the ball.

Self-determinism.

The whole tendency of modern psychology is, in fact, to elaborate and in elaborating to substantiate a doctrine put forward by Aristotle under the name of self-determinism. According to this doctrine we are determined, not by natural forces nor by an external environment, but by ourselves, that is by forces and tendencies operating within us, yet operating beyond the bounds of our consciousness. These forces and tendencies determine the strength and the nature of our conscious desires.

A man, as Aristotle says, comes to have a good character because he has continually performed good acts. But he cannot continually perform good acts unless he is the sort of man whose nature it is to perform them, unless, that is to say, he has the good character from which the good acts necessarily spring. This character will, in its turn, proceed from and be formed by a preceding series of good acts. Retracing our steps by this method over the past history of the individual, we assert that the actions which he performs at any given moment spring from, and are conditioned by, his being the sort of person that he is at the moment, and further that he is the particular sort of person that he then is because of the impulses which he experiences and the tendencies which he exhibits. If, therefore, we go far enough back, we can show that the tendencies and impulses which were originally his on the first occasion on which he acted are those which really determine the whole subsequent tenor of his life. Psycho-analysis has done little more than dot the i's and cross the t's of this doctrine. It represents human beings not as drawn from in front but as pushed from behind; as motivated, that is to say, not by a rational desire to achieve ends and to fulfil purposes envisaged by the imagination as desirable, but as impelled by a drive from behind whose strength is derived from forces which are both incalculable and irrational. In so doing psycho-analysis undermines the reason no less than the will.

B. IRRATIONALISM

Nineteenth-Century View of Reason.

It is interesting to compare the modern attitude to reason and reasoning with that of the nineteenth century.

Our fathers, taking an optimistic view of themselves as of the world as a whole, believed that they were reasonable beings. This belief involved two corollaries. In the first place, reason was free. Its deliverances might be, and no doubt in practice frequently were, biased by prejudice and distorted by desire; but the fact that reason could be deflected by these influences was a temporary defect due to man's incomplete evolution. It was, indeed, a basic assumption of the age that reason in theory could, and in practice often did, operate freely. It could arrive at an impartial and 'reasoned' choice between alternative courses of action; it could take a disinterested survey of evidence with a view to forming a 'reasoned' conclusion or belief. It was only in so far as men's reasons operated 'freely' in choosing and believing that they could be said to act and think 'rationally'. Fortunately, however, they had already reached a stage of evolution at which appeals to their 'free reason' were sometimes successful, and, under influence of education and other enlightening forces, the degree of their 'rationality' might be expected continually to increase. In the second place, reason was an instrument for reaching truth. One might of course make mistakes, argue faultily or jump to unjustifiable conclusions, but the mistakes could be detected, the faulty arguments corrected, the unjustifiable conclusions revised. This process of detection, correction and revision was itself the work of reason. Hence, if reason went wrong, it was only by reasoning—better reasoning, that is to say—that it could be set right. But, whatever mistakes it might make and however inadequate it might be as an instrument for reaching truth, it was always open to reason to arrive at conclusions which were true. A true conclusion was one which corresponded with external facts, and it was because of this correspondence that it was true. Thus the freedom of reason and its truth-reaching properties went hand in hand. A free reason was one that was constrained only by the evidence, the evidence of the facts; when, and only when, it was so constrained, it arrived at conclusions which were true.

The view that reason was free and that it could reach true conclusions was fundamental in nineteenth-century thought. J. S. Mill, for example, to take a typical representative of the time, tells us of his father that 'so complete was my father's reliance on the influence of reason over the minds of mankind, whenever it is allowed to reach them, that he felt as if all would be gained if the whole population were taught to read, if all sorts of opinions were allowed to be addressed to them by word and in writing, and if by means of a suffrage they could nominate a legislature to give effect to the opinions they adopted.'[1] Truth, in other words, will out, if men's minds are only given a fair chance to find it; for, being reasonable by nature, men have only to be given access to truth to recognise it. And, speaking of himself and his friends, J. S. Mill goes on to say that what they 'principally thought of, was to alter other people's opinions; to make them believe according to evidence, and know what was their real interest, which, when they knew, they would, we thought, by the instrument of opinion, enforce a regard to it upon one another.'[2]

Changed attitude of Twentieth Century.

I do not think that I can better convey the change that has come over the intellectual climate of our age in regard to its attitude to reason than by saying that both these quotations, which passed without comment in the nineteenth, would be immediately questioned in the twentieth century. Twentieth-century thought no longer assumes either that men will embrace the truth when they see it, or that they will alter their opinions because reasonable grounds are adduced for their doing so. And this assumption is no longer made, because men to-day are fundamentally sceptical of the part played by reason in determining our conduct and forming our beliefs. Reason, it is widely suggested, is a mere tool or handmaid

[1] J. S. Mill. *Autobiography*, p. 89 (World's Classics edition).
[2] J. S. Mill. *Autobiography*, p. 94 (World's Classics edition).

of desire. Its function is to secure the ends which we unconsciously set ourselves, by inventing excuses for what we instinctively want to do and arguments for what we instinctively want to believe. There is, in fact, at bottom very little difference between reason and faith, for, if faith be defined as the power of believing what we know to be untrue, reason is the power of kidding ourselves into believing that what we want to think is true.

To this change in the contemporary attitude to reason psycho-analysis has largely contributed. Psycho-analysts hold, as we have seen, that the forces that dominate our natures are fundamentally instinctive and, therefore, non-rational in character. The unconscious is pictured as a restless sea of instinct and impulse, a sea agitated by gusts of libido, swept by the waves of desire, threaded by the currents of urge and drive; and upon these waves and currents consciousness, with all that it contains, bobs helplessly like a cork. Consciousness is represented, in fact, as a sort of by-product of the unconscious. This general conception is exemplified by the attitude current in psycho-analytic literature to reason.

The animal origin of man and the fact that his roots are deep down in nature are emphasised; the inference is that fundamentally he is swayed by the same kind of *natural* forces as those which determine the animals. Of these *natural* forces we know very little, especially since we have succeeded in evolving reason, one of whose main functions is to rationalise them, and so disguise from us their real character. But reason is itself an expression of these instinctive *natural* forces, one of the latest and the weakest. It is a feeble shoot springing from a deep, dim foundation of unconscious strivings, and maintaining a precarious existence as their apologist and their handmaid.

Reason, in fact, is a mere tool of instinct; it is instinct which determines the occasions of its operation and its function is limited to discovering means for satisfying the instincts which employ it. Professor McDougall's theory of instinct points to the same conclusion. 'The instincts,' it will be remembered, are, on this view, 'the prime movers of all human activity . . . all the complex intellectual apparatus of the most highly developed mind is but the instrument by which these impulses seek their satisfaction.' Reason, in other words, is a mechanism; it is the engine of the personality, and instinct is the steam that sets it going. And, since reason can operate only when driven by the impulsive force of instinct, it can proceed only along the path which instinct indicates to the goal which instinct dictates.

C. REASONING AND RATIONALISING

If this is the nature and function of reason, it is, it is obvious, a misnomer to call it free. Called into action by instinct, it must needs arrive at those conclusions which instinct demands. We are accustomed in daily life to make a distinction between reasoning and rationalising. Reasoning is an honest, rationalising a dishonest use of reason. A person who reasons uses his mind to take impartial stock of the evidence, and permits his conclusions to be determined by what he finds; he does not, in other words, in so far as he is reasonable, allow the operations of his reason to be biased by his wishes or dictated by his hopes. A person who rationalises uses his reason to arrive only at those conclusions which he consciously or unconsciously desires. Paying attention to those facts which support the desired conclusion, he ignores all others. If supporting facts are wanting, he imagines them. It is rationalising when the smoker persuades himself that tobacco ash is good for the carpet, the fisherman that fish being cold-blooded creatures feel the tearing of the hook less than himself, and the British patriot that he went to war with Germany because of the violation of Belgium. Thus, while the conclusions of reasoning are determined by circumstances external to and independent of the reason, those of rationalising are determined by personal hopes and fears.

Now this distinction, if psycho-analysis is correct, cannot be upheld. For the distinction between reasoning and rationalising is itself a product of rationalising, the offspring of our desire to think that our reasons are or can be free.

Freud's later theories.

I have already mentioned the interpretation which Freud places upon the more recently evolved capacities of the human spirit, and upon the experiences which they involve; religion, science, art and thought are, he holds, activities of compensation. It is impossible to read any of Freud's later books without being struck by the ingenuity he displays in exhibiting apparently disinterested rational activities as the sublimated versions of instinctive desires or as the compensation for instinctive renunciations.

I have already referred to the treatment of religion as arising from the child's feeling of helplessness in a hostile world, and from the longing for a guiding and protecting father which that feeling evokes to supply the place of the earthly father whose power, as the child grows up, is seen to decline and whose interest in the child is felt to wane. Morality, again, is a device on the part of society to secure compliance with the unnatural demands which living in society makes upon the individual.

To realise how such conceptions of religion and morality originate, it is necessary to understand something of Freud's later theories. These constitute a distinct advance upon his earlier position, an advance which is also an elaboration. There is, for example, a distinction between the 'ego' consciousness of the child and that of the adult. The former is a bundle of diffused sensations which are coextensive with the child's world. It is only by experience that the child learns to separate those of his sensations which come from an independent, external world which he is unable to control, from those which, being internally aroused, he can make for himself. The separation leads to a distinction between the self and the world, a distinction which leads to a contraction of the 'ego', so that the diffused, vague 'ego-consciousness' of the child becomes the narrow, sharply defined 'ego-consciousness' of the adult.

Nevertheless, the memory of the wider consciousness of childhood still survives in the unconscious, and survives encircled by a halo of regret. The idea associated with this loved memory is an idea of just that limitless extension and oneness with the universe which has often been regarded as the core of the religious feeling.

Freud's attitude to Morality.

Freud's attitude to morality springs from his conception of an ever recurrent duel between civilisation and instinct. In his later books Freud introduces important distinctions between three aspects or parts of the personality, the 'ego', the 'super-ego' and the 'id'. The id is the unconscious, instinctive part of our natures, the ego is the self of which we are normally conscious, the super-ego the conception of the self which is imposed upon the 'ego' by culture and civilisation. The super-ego is what the 'ego' would like to be in its role of a fully cultivated and civilised adult, what in its more optimistic moments the ego conceives itself as in fact being, what, indeed, it must be, if it is to fit smoothly into the framework of civilisation; it is the ego putting up, as it were, a good show before the neighbours.

In its effort to realise the super-ego, the ego is hindered by the solicitations of the primitive and unregenerate id. For such realisation involves the continual thwarting and suppression of the id's instinctive desires. This suppression grows in severity as civilisation grows in complexity, with the resultant neuroses which Freud's therapeutic method seeks to resolve.

Now it is by means of morality that civilisation brings the id to heel. Inevitably, in imposing its demands, the super-ego in the form of conscience pays too little attention to the happiness of the ego and the instinctive cravings of the id.

'It . . . does not trouble enough about the mental condition of human beings; it enjoins a command and never asks whether or not it is possible for them to obey it. It presumes on the contrary that a man's ego is psychologically capable of anything that is required of it—that his ego has unlimited power over his id.'[1]

In this conception we find at once the root of civilisation's discontents and the goal of the Freudian method, which, by moderating the demands of the super-ego, seeks to alleviate them. Beauty, cleanliness, order, intellectual activity and social relations are all examined from this point of view, and diagnosed as at once sublimations of and sops to the instinctive demands of the id. Just as Marxists interpret the course of human history in terms of the different techniques of production by means of which men have satisfied their material needs, so Freud suggests an interpretation of human thought and culture in terms of the different ways by which they have sought to compensate themselves for the instinctive sacrifices which living in society involves. I do not mean that he has so interpreted it himself; but he has consistently maintained the fruitfulness of such interpretation and indicated the lines on which it would proceed.

Belittlement of Reason.

These various currents of thought tend in each case to the same conclusion; that is, to the belittlement of reason and its subservience to other parts of our nature. Reason, it seems, is a mere tool for reaching those conclusions to which our instincts prompt us.[2] The beliefs we hold are not the result of an impartial survey of the evidence, but

---

[1] Freud. *Civilisation and its Discontents,* p. 139.

[2] Freud himself was very far from being a disparager of reason and often seems unaware of the 'irrationalist' implications of his theories. Thus we find him announcing that 'the domination of reason would prove to be the strongest unifying force among men.' How this can be possible, if reason is a determined by-product of non-rational elements and forces, is very far from being clear.

are reflections of the fundamental desires and tendencies of our nature. We believe what we do upon instinct; but we have also an instinct to use our reason to find arguments in support of our beliefs. Reason, it seems, is suborned from the first; she can dance only to the tune which instinct pipes her. The higher activities of the human spirit are not enjoyed on merits; they are the sops which man has invented to salve the instincts which have been wounded by his renunciations. They do not, therefore, express or point to anything in the nature of things. Morality is not a recognition of an intrinsic difference between rightness and wrongness, of which conscience is the arbiter. Conscience, as Freud puts it, is merely 'the result of instinctual renunciation'.[1] Art is not an acknowledgment of a beauty in the world which the artist seeks to catch and to reproduce, religion of an underlying reality to which man may hope to penetrate and of a purpose which he may hope to fulfil; they are merely the by-products of unconscious urges in ourselves. When these urges are denied satisfaction through normal channels, they are diverted into new ones, and religion and art are the result. These are not the windows through which men gaze out upon the real world; they are the safety valves through which their thwarted urges let off steam. As for thought, it is a means of justifying our fallacies and sealing them with our approval. 'I am sure only of one thing, that the judgments of value made by mankind are immediately determined by their desires for happiness; in other words, that their judgments are attempts to prop up their illusions with arguments.'[2] It is difficult to resist the temptation of asking whether this conviction applies to the judgment by which it is affirmed.

[1] Freud. *Civilisation and its Discontents*, p. 114.
[2] Freud. *Civilisation and its Discontents*, p. 143.

III

EFFECTS UPON CONTEMPORARY THOUGHT

Adequately to trace the effects of these implications of psycho-analytic theory in the thought, the art and the literature of the times would be a formidable task; nor can it be attempted here. The subject demands a book to itself. Some account of the more obvious effects may, however, be not inappropriately included within the scope of this one. I have classified under the names 'Determinism' and 'Irrationalism' the main implications of the doctrines of modern psychology. There are certain familiar tendencies of contemporary thought which clearly group themselves under these two heads. It is to these that I propose to refer very briefly here, devoting a final chapter to the influence of modern psychology upon contemporary literature.

It would, I think, be generally agreed that among the distinguishing characteristics of modern thought may be included scepticism, anti-authoritarianism, fatalism, and an insistence upon the right to the unfettered enjoyment of the pleasures of the moment. It is not difficult to show that each of these tendencies is encouraged, if it is not actually prompted, by the doctrines I have sketched.

Scepticism.

Scepticism, it is obvious, is a direct result of the view of reason suggested by Freud's work. If reason is merely a tool of our instincts, there is no presumption that it will give us truth. Admittedly it arrives at those beliefs which we unconsciously wish to think true; but there is no reason why the universe should conform to our unconscious wishes, or why what we passionately desire to be the case should be the case.

Formerly men made a distinction between their judgments—those of them, at least, which they believed to be rational—and their wishes. Rational judgments were thought to be founded on evidence, and, in so far as they conformed to it, to provide a secure basis for knowledge and prediction. Wishes may father thoughts but they do not breed evidence. Hence, it has always been considered the mark of a rational man to distinguish between his judgments of probability and his hopes and wishes. But, if his judgments of probability are themselves the offspring of his hopes and wishes, the distinction must be abandoned. The only test of a true belief now becomes the pragmatic test of its ability to satisfy the wishes which led us to form it. Since a belief which has been satisfactory in this respect in the past may cease to be so owing to a change in circumstances, or in the unconscious wishes which led to its formation, no belief can be more than provisionally and temporarily true. The intellect in fact is not an instrument for divining truth; its function is to provide reasons for thinking that our wishes will be gratified and our instinctive beliefs verified. This it does by persuading us, or most of us, that the universe is fundamentally spiritual and purposive in character. As such, it will be friendly to our aspirations and comfortable with our beliefs. Most thinkers have accordingly felt convinced that it is both. Since, however, this conviction is merely a rationalisation of our beliefs, there is no reason to trust it. This scepticism in regard to the conclusions of reason accords very well with the attitude to reason adopted by some modern physicists which I outlined in Chapter IV.[1]

Eddington, Jeans and others suggest, as we have seen, that the world which physics studies is not the real world but an abstraction from it. The process of abstraction is performed by reason, which selects certain aspects and qualities of reality for treatment and ignores those with which it is unable to deal. The conclusions of science are not, therefore, directly revelatory of reality, which, it is suggested, may be more directly and truly revealed in the inspiration of the artist or the insight of the saint. In

[1] Chapter IV, pp. 74–77, 98–102; see also Chapter V, p. 123.

this respect physics and psychology join forces to engender a certain scepticism in regard to the conclusions of reason. The instrument of knowledge may, it seems, itself be defective.

Anti-authoritarianism.

But because reason may be a faulty guide, it does not, therefore, follow that we should return to authority.

Psycho-analysis shows fairly conclusively that the wish to exercise power over others is one of the most fundamental drives of the unconscious. It is a wish which sublimates itself in various ways, and justifies itself by many different rationalisations such as 'the divine right of kings', 'the majesty of the law', parental authority, or clerical dogmatism. Yet in all these forms authority is only a cloak for the desire to impose our will on other people. Once the psychological basis of authority is exposed, its prestige is impaired. We might obey the priest when we thought his authority backed by the power and informed by the wisdom of God; but the obligation to obedience is undermined when it is exhibited to us as a sublimated desire to control men's minds by deterring them from using their reasons.

Hence arises a general distrust of authority in the modern world, not only the traditional authority of priest and king, mandarin and magistrate, but of all the self-constituted pundits, experts, philosophers, scientists, prophets and reformers who aspire to take their places.

What Walter Lippmann, in a striking phrase, has called 'the acids of modernity' have not only proved corrosive of the traditional authorities of the past, but seem likely to prove equally effective against any new-found authority in the future. Science, as we have seen, substitutes hypothesis for conclusion; religion has lost the old dogmatic assurance, or, in so far as it retains it, palpably loses hold on the modern mind; art is frankly experimental, while in the sphere of morals the contemporary generation increasingly refuses to subscribe to the sexual restraints and taboos of the last.

Many forces no doubt have contributed to this fluidity of code and thought, a fluidity which seems to many to be indistinguishable from anarchy; but not least among them is that exposure of the root of the authoritarian impulse itself which psycho-analysis is considered to have effected. Men subscribe to creeds and observe rules and prohibitions more willingly when they believe them to be the embodiments of inspiration and the expression of revealed truth than when they regard them as sublimations of the impulse to power.

Fatalism.

Upon the fatalistic tendencies of the new psychology I have already commented in connection with the treatment of conscience and the will. If the will is not really the freely exercised faculty that it appears to be, efforts at self-control are not within our control. If our characters are made for us, not by us, regret for our deficiencies is as idle as pride in our virtues is unjustified. To hold that our characters are what our past has made them, that our actions are the fruits of our complexes, and that our interests in impersonal things, our hobbies, our holidays, even our choice of a profession, are ways of resolving them, is to hold that we are not free. Even our efforts to correct the tendencies we regret are the expression of forces for which we are no more responsible than for the tendencies. If, then, we can neither build our characters nor mould our lives, if we are as powerless to control the future as to modify the past, we may as well make the best of life as it is and take what comes to us without striving to have it different.

Thus a fourth characteristic of the contemporary attitude to life which is traceable to modern psychology is the tendency to make the most of the present moment, to live in and for the present. If the future is not only unknown but beyond our control, it is the part of wisdom, so it is said, to make the best of the present which we know.

Practical Epicureanism.

Where everything is uncertain, the doctrine of let us eat and drink for to-morrow we die, at once concrete and definite, is eagerly embraced. Such an attitude, whatever it may mean for a mature sage, involves for the youth of the twentieth century a contemptuous abandonment of those inhibitions and restraints which the nineteenth century complacently termed its 'morals'. At the same time, the prohibitions of traditional ethics, deprived of their supernatural backing, lose their accustomed force. We should be good, we used to be told, because goodness is pleasing to God. He loves an upright man; he also likes him to be temperate and continent. Once the practice of virtue is identified with pleasing God, it becomes difficult to say how much so-called virtuous conduct has been prompted by the desire to achieve an eternity of celestial bliss, and to avoid an eternity of infernal torment.

It is notorious to-day that heavenly rewards no longer attract and infernal punishments no longer deter with their pristine force; many people are frankly derisive of both, and, seeing no prospect of divine compensation in the next world for the wine and kisses that morality bids them eschew in this one, take more or less unanimously to the wine and kisses.

But psycho-analysis has affected man's attitude to the actual moment of passing experience more directly than through the scepticism which it has engendered in regard to the traditional, inhibitory morality. To distrust of the old doctrines of prudence and prohibition it adds a positive doctrine of the obligation to experiment. It says not merely that it is not worth while to deny ourselves to save the soul, but that it is our duty to spend the soul. Psycho-analysis is responsible, in other words, for a positive creed of self-expression. To thwart an instinctive drive, to stifle an unconscious desire is, Freud has taught, to injure the personality at its very root. Nobody has shown more conclusively than he has done how much of the hysteria, the neurosis and the vague self-dissatisfaction of modern life is due to the repression of natural desires in youth. And not only hysteria and neurosis, but the Puritanism which sees in prohibition the whole duty of man, and equates virtue with self-denial. Such morality he has exhibited as a rationalisation of the envy of those who, themselves starved of pleasure, cannot tolerate the enjoyment of others. This aspect of his teaching has achieved widespread notoriety, with the result that many young people regard self-expression as a primary duty, and count repression, at least in theory, as the only sin.

The Youth Movements of the modern world are visibly affected by this new morality. Leisure, they hold, should be utilised for enjoyment, enjoyment which depends not upon the efforts of other people, upon entertainers paid to provide amusement, but which consists in and arises from the free expression of one's own spirit. Dancing and singing are forms of such expression, reflecting the rhythms of our being which underlie consciousness. Hence, what seems to the traditionalist to be mere frivolity is regarded by many young people to-day as the serious business of life. While the ultimate purpose of life may be doubtful, this, at least, they hold to be clear, that we should enjoy the present and express and develop our natures. Hence enjoyment and self-expression come to be regarded as ends in themselves, and not merely as means to greater efficiency in work. We should, it is urged, refresh the spirit for its own sake and not as a preparation for the duties and business of life. Refreshment of the spirit *is* the business of life. The same attitude expresses itself in a new conception of the sexual impulse. By the belief that this should be utilised not merely for the procreation of children but for the expression of personality, for the enrichment of the spirit by the intimacy of the contacts it brings, and above all for sheer enjoyment, this generation is perhaps more than in any other single respect distinguished from the last.

Praise of the new morality.

It is impossible not to approve of many of these manifestations of the modern spirit. In the last century, it is now obvious, men and women muffled and starved their personalities. Pleasure they regarded with distrust, nor did it occur to them that enjoyment was an adequate motive for activity. They equated duty with the restraint of all impulses except the impulse to self-restraint; such as could not be restrained they rationalised. The Victorians were adepts at rationalising their impulses; they beat their children 'for their children's good', and made profits out of the backward peoples upon whom they believed themselves to be bestowing the boons of Christianity and civilisation. They regarded this profitable process as a sacred duty, and talked of the 'White man's burden'.[1] They could not even indulge their impulse to adventure without justifying themselves with a sound utilitarian reason; they explored the Antarctic in order to look for coal beds, and climbed the Himalayas to make meteorological observations. As Samuel Butler says of his father, they would never admit that they did anything because they wanted to. To use Freud's terminology, the unconsciousnesses of such a generation must have been very festering pits of corruption, dustbins into which were shot all the desires to which one was afraid to own in public, hotbeds of thwarted impulses.

Into this noisome chamber modern psychology has let light and air. It has come with the effect of a housemaid who enters a room too long closed, opens the shutters and uses a vigorous broom to sweep away the cobwebs. As the dust escapes out of the window, the room becomes cleaner, sweeter, healthier. And there can, I think, be no reasonable doubt that partly

[1] See *Victoriana*, compiled by Barton and Sitwell *passim* and especially quotations from the Earl of Carnarvon on China (p. 60), Sir Charles Napier on the mountain tribes of Scinde (p. 30) and Gladstone (almost any quotation).

as the result of the influence of modern psychology, men and women to-day are franker, more open, less hypocritical. They know more about the conditions of psychological health and more about themselves; they are less easily taken in by the self-assumed authority of others, and they are apt at unmasking the egotism which underlies the officially altruistic utterances of eminent persons. Modern psychology has pricked the bubble of the rhetorical period and taken the colour out of the purple patch. Finally, the insistence on the importance of self-expression may well lead to a renaissance of art, as it has already led to a renaissance of community dancing and singing.

Criticism of the New Psychology.

But, while so much stands to the credit side of the new psychology, the debit is serious. Scepticism in regard to the intellect and fatalism in regard to conduct have a devitalising effect, sapping energy and initiative and discouraging that intellectual curiosity which, responsible for modern science, is responsible also for psycho-analysis itself.

Psycho-analysis has led to a belittlement of the more lately evolved characteristics of the human spirit, and by exhibiting their dependence upon the earlier, to an interest in, which in some cases has become a glorification of, the savage and the primitive. More important is the fact that it has engendered a distrust of reason which has led men to glorify unreason, to seek in instinct a short cut to truth and in impulse a sure guide to conduct. As an unrepentant rationalist, who believes that reason is not only free but man's only guide to truth and only hope for the future, I venture, therefore, to suggest here a doubt whether the implications traced in this chapter do in fact follow from the doctrines which psycho-analysis has advanced. I do not wish to criticise these doctrines; criticism, indeed, is not my purpose in this book which is concerned with exposition, but it may be pertinent to inquire whether they necessitate the construction which has been placed upon them.

Do the implications follow?

Let us, in the first place, apply to the psycho-analytic view of reason the arguments which were used in Chapter III, in criticism of the Behaviourist position;[1] let us, that is to say, push the views of psycho-analysts to their *reductio ad absurdum.*

If it is in fact the case that our thoughts are not free but are dictated by our wishes, and that reasoning is, therefore, mere rationalising, then the conclusion applies also to the reasoning of psycho-analysis. This too is a mere rationalisation of the desire to believe that human nature is of a certain kind and motivated in a certain way. As such it has no necessary relation to fact; it merely reflects a certain condition of the psychologist's unconscious. This is not to say that it is necessarily untrue; merely to point out that it is meaningless to ask whether it is true or not. Truth implies correspondence—correspondence, that is, between the belief which claims to be true and the fact which makes it true. But, if psycho-analysis is correct, our beliefs have no external reference at all; they are merely intellectualised versions of our wishes. To ask if a belief is true is, therefore, as meaningless as to ask whether an emotion is true; all that one is entitled to say is that the belief is held. Since, therefore, it seems to follow that, if psycho-analysis is correct in what it asserts about reason, it is meaningless to ask whether psycho-analysis is true, there is no reason to suppose that it is correct in what it asserts about reason. In other words, if the psycho-analytic account of reason is justified, there is no reason to take it seriously. If, on the other hand, there is no reason to take it seriously, the grounds for supposing that reason is not free and can never reach objective truth disappear.

[1] *See* p. 57.

To refuse to take it seriously means that we must be willing to regard the theories of psycho-analysis as springing from a free and impartial consideration of the evidence, as propounded: in other words, for no other reason than that they are seen to be in accordance with fact. But if the psycho-analyst can reason disinterestedly in accordance with fact, so can other people. Hence the view of reason, as being *always* the mere tool of instinct, must be abandoned. What is wanted is a principle which will enable us to distinguish the cases in which reason is working freely from those in which it is merely rationalising our wishes. But such a principle is not so far forthcoming.

Illegitimate distinctions between faculties.

In the second place, it may be doubted whether the separation, which psycho-analysis introduces, within the personality between different faculties such as reason, will and instinct, is really justified; whether, indeed, the sharp distinction between consciousness and the unconscious can itself be sustained. What is valuable in modern psychology is its insistence on the purposive character of living activity. For a psychology of atomic, psychical units acting upon and being acted upon by each other, based upon a mechanism which is becoming increasingly unworkable in the physical sciences, it substitutes a spontaneous, creative impulsion which is the essence of all vital behaviour. This impulsion is purposive in the sense that it can be adequately interpreted only in terms of the goal which it is seeking to realise.

Where psycho-analysis seems open to objection is in regard to the distinctions which it tends to introduce within the impulsion itself—distinctions which result in a differentiation of the human psyche into different faculties, and in particular in a separation between instinct and reason. As the result of this separation, reason tends to be represented as a mere tool of instinct, employed to achieve ends which are not its own. A better way is to regard living activity as single and continuous in and through all expressions of itself, these expressions being differentiated solely in terms of the ends to which they are directed. It is the same living activity which moves us to acquire food when we are hungry and to discover the differential calculus when we are inquisitive. In fact, man is chiefly to be distinguished from the animals in virtue of the different ends to which the impulsion of the living activity, the same in him as it is in them, prompts him.

Application of conclusions reached in two previous chapters.

Evolution is a process which transforms the subconscious cravings and blind urges of the animal into the intelligent foresight and rational motivation of the human being; such, at least, is the view urged in the preceding two chapters. It is a corollary of this view that the qualities of spontaneity and creativity which characterise human activity at its lowest levels still characterise it at its higher. A man is as free when he acts reasonably as when he acts instinctively, as much his own master when he pursues abstract knowledge as when he breaks the furniture in a rage. Reason, in fact, is not something tacked on to instinct; still less is it a tool which instinct has evolved. It is simple instinct at a higher level, directed upon novel ends. In other words, it is possible to desire a thing *per se* because it is the reasonable thing to desire, and to hold a belief because in all the circumstances it is the rational belief to hold. In fact a being may be defined as reasonable just in so far as he does so desire, act, and believe.

Along these lines it seems possible to maintain the view of life as a self-determining, dynamic, creative agency, without thereby degrading reason to the status of a mechanical tool of irrational instincts. In my view, it is only on some such lines as these that, in the light of modern psychology, the freedom of reason can be vindicated. But such a view is based not upon the deterministic implications of psycho-analysis, but rather upon the concept of life as a dynamic spontaneous force or principle, which was sketched in the last chapter but one. Applying this view to the questions which have been raised in the present chapter, we may sum up the implications of modern psychology by saying that it has led us to concede a far greater importance to the undercurrent of instinct and impulse in our lives than did the nineteenth century; to accept the fact that non-rational influences may bias and distort reason to a hitherto unsuspected extent, and to realise that, since these influences cannot always be detected, it is extremely difficult to allow for them. What is important is that, while recognising the fundamentally dynamic character of life and its continuity in all living beings, we should not lend countenance to the somewhat derogatory attitude to its highest expressions in will and reason for which psycho-analysis has been in some quarters responsible.

CHAPTER IX

THE INVASION OF LITERATURE
BY PSYCHOLOGY

Introductory.

I propose in this chapter to try to trace some of the effects of the tendencies described in the last on contemporary literature. I wish to make it clear at the outset that I am not proposing to embark upon a general account of modern literature; I am concerned with it only in so far as it exhibits tendencies illustrative of an attitude to human personality for which the influence of the psychological views I have outlined is largely responsible. I shall, therefore, limit my treatment to those characteristics of modern literature which illustrate and exemplify the psychological theories already described. I shall also confine myself to the novel, not only because the novel is the most characteristic form of modern literature, but also because it most clearly displays the tendencies with which I am concerned.

Importance of Characters in Victorian Novels.

The relevant characteristics of the modern novel may most suitably be described in relation to those of the Victorian novel with which they are contrasted. The great triumph of the Victorian novelists lay in their ability to create characters, and it is the absence of memorable and outstanding characters which constitutes the chief difference between the Victorian novel and the modern.

The Victorian novels, it is obvious, stand or fall by their characters, and on the whole they triumphantly stand. Thackeray and Dickens, George Eliot and the Brontës, Trollope and Mrs. Gaskell, to take a few names at random, all possessed the gift of creating characters.

Their books teem with real live people, as round and rich and vital as their flesh and blood prototypes, more so in fact than many of them, and Weller and Micawber, Becky Sharp and Mrs. Poyser, Heathcliffe and Paul Emmanuel and Mrs. Proudie are among the most memorable achievements of fiction in any age or country.

By their characters the Victorian novelists set great store. They rarely introduce them without a preliminary flourish of descriptive matter, and even comparatively unimportant personages usually get a page or two to themselves, describing their lineage, appearance, personal characteristics, likes, dislikes, attitude to religion, to morals, to their friends and neighbours, and to life generally, before they are allowed to take the stage and we to make their acquaintance. Take, for example, the introduction of Mrs. Corney, widow and matron of the workhouse in *Oliver Twist*. Mrs. Corney is not an important character although a very amusing one, and her relations with Mr. Bumble are a side issue in the book, having little relevance to the main theme; yet in my edition of *Oliver Twist* two pages are devoted to a preliminary description of herself, her room at the workhouse, her meditation upon her late and hopes of a future husband, her preparations for tea. . . . Or take Mr. Podsnap in *Our Mutual Friend*. Mr. Podsnap is unessential to the story; he plays no part in the unfolding of the complicated plot; he is introduced only in order that Dickens may speak his mind on the subject of English hypocrisy, complacency and unimaginative insularity; and speak his mind he does to the tune of three pages devoted to the introduction of Mr. Podsnap, before Mr. Podsnap is allowed to speak for himself.

This elaborate introduction of the characters, symptomatic of the importance of the place which they occupy in the novel, is characteristic of all the great Victorian writers. Trollope, the last writer in the grand and leisurely Victorian manner, keeps up the tradition to the end. In *The Last Chronicle of Barset* there are two single ladies, the Misses Prettyman, who keep a girls' school. They are introduced in a chapter generally descriptive of people living at Silverbridge where the main scenes of the book are laid, and, except for one or two incidental appearances, they are not heard of again. Yet two charming and elaborate pages are devoted to a description of their tastes, habits, hopes, reputation in the town, and the small differences of temperament between the two. The characters introduced with so much elaboration triumphantly justify the care bestowed upon them. They live with amazing vitality; for them, and them alone, are the novels of the last century still read and re-read. And, once introduced, they are secure of a place in the reader's mind; for they are pre-eminently memorable.

Absence of Characters in the Modern Novel.

Now an array of memorable characters is precisely what the modern novel does not provide. Every now and then a writer of genius may throw off a character who lives on in one's memory. Wells's Aunt Susan for instance in *Tono Bungay*, or Arnold Bennett's Elsie in *Riceyman's Steps*; but these are the rare exceptions rather than the rule, and, when we come to the most modern writers, Joyce and Lawrence, Huxley and Virginia Woolf, the memorable character has disappeared altogether. It is difficult to remember so much as the names of any of the personages in these later books.

To point out that the Victorians created memorable characters but that the moderns do not, is not to say that the moderns are necessarily inferior to the Victorians. The disparity arises less from inferiority of talent than from difference of aim.

The Edwardian writers, for example, were concerned less with men and women than with movements and causes. Their aim was, often avowedly, propagandist, and they introduced individual men and women into their stories only in so far as they served to expound a creed, to point a moral, or to illustrate an abuse. Even in those novels which are not directly written with a purpose the element of propaganda is still present. In the first few pages of Wells's *History of Mr. Polly*, for instance, usually regarded as the high-spirited offspring of an exuberant imagination written for the sheer fun of the thing, there is an attack upon the elementary educational system which for sheer virulence of abuse and directness of reformist purpose is unequalled. Inevitably in such books the individuals tended to be types rather than individuals; their value from the novelist's point of view lies not, as did that of the Victorian characters, in their differences from but in their resemblances to others similarly situated, in their typicality rather than in their idiosyncrasy.

Victorian Characters as selections.

If the Edwardian novelist used the novel as a vehicle of social reform, seeking to arouse the indignation and to quicken the conscience of the reader by the presentation of social anomalies, the Georgian and especially the post-war writers narrow their scope, and concentrate their attention upon the individual himself.

When we contrast the men and women portrayed by these later writers with their Victorian predecessors, we cannot avoid being struck by the fact that the memorableness of the Victorian characters is largely achieved by means of a process of rigid selection. Each character embodies two or three dominant characteristics and no more. Whatever might interfere with our perception of these characteristics and blur the outlines of the simple clear-cut portrait is ruthlessly excluded. Hence, the Victorian characters stand out in relief, because they are reached by process of abstraction. Mr. Micawber is always incompetent and optimistic, the child wife of David Copperfield incompetent and foolish, Becky Sharp competent and unscrupulous. In extreme cases the character makes one or two appropriate remarks, which express the characteristic of the character, and which become so conventional that they may be regarded Behaviouristically as responses to stimuli, like the words uttered by talking dolls when they are squeezed in the right places. 'I have never deserted Mr. Micawber,' says Mrs. Micawber, 'and I never will,' and to all intents and purposes she never says anything else.

Thus nineteenth-century characters approximate very closely to the Humours of the Elizabethan drama. Each is or represents a particular aspect of human nature; none are whole people. In this sense, if one wishes to be impolite, one may dub them caricatures.

Again, nineteenth-century characters do not, speaking broadly, develop. What they were at the beginning of the book, that with unimportant modifications they are at the end. Heathcliffe, Micawber, Uriah Heep, Amelia Sedley, Fred Bayham, Mrs. Proudie and the rest do not change; if they did, they would not be so vivid and clear cut; they would not, in a word, be so memorable. 'I have never deserted Mr. Micawber' is Mrs. Micawber's sign-manual, the special noise by which she is to be recognised all through the book, as if a clock-work doll had been wound up to say its appointed piece. She is saying it at the end, as she said it at the beginning, and thus it is that infallibly we remember Mrs. Micawber. In this sense nineteenth-century characters are static, not dynamic.

But to say that they are static, to say even that they are caricatures is not necessarily to be impolite to their creators. It is simply to express one's sense of recognition of a different aim from that which inspires the moderns.

The aims of the moderns.

For, while the object of the nineteenth-century novelist is to create memorable characters, to point a moral or to adorn a tale, the modern writer's chief concern is to find out exactly what people are like, and to record his discoveries. His purpose is psychological research;

he wants to get at all that there is in any individual, and in conducting his researches he discovers, what, of course, is obvious, that human beings are not simple, far less simple in fact than the characters in Victorian novels. Victorian characters, when they are not downright heroes and villains, are generally composed of few elements, of which the good preponderate notably over the bad, or vice versa, so that the reader is never left in any doubt, by the time he reaches the end of the book, which are the nice people and which are not.

Now real people are not just good and bad; they are not even simple mixtures in which the balance of virtuous and vicious elements can be readily struck. They are not, if modern psychology is right, composed of elements, known as qualities, at all. A human being, psychology teaches, is more like a river than a bundle of qualities; running now fast now slow, now clear now turbid, he presents a different surface at every moment. Capable at one moment of supreme heroisms, he is guilty at another of incredible meannesses. And, as with individuals, so also with the relations between them. In a Victorian novel a man's intentions towards an attractive woman are apt to be either virtuous or the reverse; in fact, however, every love affair is composed of elements of gold and of clay, of sunlight and of savagery, while in a busy man's life women are alternately blown aloft like soap bubbles or jettisoned as lumber.

Now it is clear that, if you set out to convey the whole variety of contradictory moods and impulses which is a person, entering with other persons similarly constituted into relations which inevitably reflect the shifting characteristics of their constituents, you will not produce a straightforward tale in which clear-cut personages, reacting according to their natures, play their appointed and predictable parts. On the contrary, your story will be unimportant, your characters scarcely remembered. Ordinary people are not memorable, and, in seeking to convey exactly what for an ordinary person the business of being alive is like, you will have to reconcile yourself to sacrificing memorableness to truth.

The demand for complexity.

The reader, if he is as modern as the author, will, on the whole, applaud the sacrifice.

People's minds to-day are more subtle than they were sixty years ago, and make greater demands in the way of subtlety upon those who cater for them. They do not expect the characters about whom they read to exhibit the old ethical simplicity, and they no longer regard a record of what people do as the most important information to be conveyed about them. The inner life, it is increasingly realised, may be more important than the outer, and the strife between conflicting elements in the same person more vivid than strife between persons. So much, at least, is implied by the suggestion that the novelist should seek to portray *all* that there is in a man, a suggestion which resolves itself on analysis into the demand that the business of the novelist is to portray life—life, that is, as it is experienced by those engaged in living it.

It is in the attempts which have been made to carry out this suggestion and to meet this demand, that the influence of modern psychological ideas may be most clearly discerned. Inevitably the attempts have been in large part experimental, and not all by any means have succeeded. The development of the modern novel is the record of these attempts. Always novelists are seeking to get nearer to life as it is actually experienced by those engaged in living it, and, as they try first one method and then another, literature is found to approach ever more closely to psychology; so much so, that novels which represent the tendency in its more extreme developments give the impression of having been written with the express purpose of illustrating the theories of psychologists and psycho-analysts. As the development proceeds, a number of different phases may be distinguished.

Literary Experiments. (1) *The biographical novel.*

The psychological movement in literature begins with a succession of biographical novels. Dispensing with plot, as the nineteenth century understood the word, novelists took as the theme of the novel the history of a single personage. The reader was presented with a series of pictures portraying the successive stages of his development. He was seen in the cradle, defying his nurse, loving his mother, resenting his father, going for the first time to school, at school, at the University, 'getting' religion, falling in love, married, divorced, remarried, unsuccessful, successful,. dead. Everything, the view seems to have been, is suitable for literary treatment, everything has its place in the novel, just as it has in life. Hence the novel tended to become a rag-bag of incidents and impressions linked together by nothing but the developing personality of the hero. J. D. Beresford's famous trilogy of *Jacob Stahl*, Compton Mackenzie's *Sinister Street*, Hugh Walpole's *Fortitude* are typical examples in this *genre*.

(2) *Putting everything in.*

The heyday of the biographical novel was in the years immediately preceding the war. During the war years, however, a further development was pending. It was found that, if the object of the writer was to put literally everything in, a single life was too large a canvas to be covered. Dorothy Richardson had, indeed, tried the experiment of extending the story of a single life through a number of successive volumes. Eleven separate volumes of her work have already appeared, the latest, up to the time of writing, *Clear Horizon*, having been published in the autumn of 1935. *Pilgrimage*, which is the record of the life of Miriam Henderson, is in many ways a remarkable work, but the narrative proceeds with almost unendurable slowness; and after nine volumes Miriam has only reached early middle age. It is, indeed, on reflection obvious that if, in pursuance of the endeavour to represent life as such, it is claimed that anything and everything that occurs must be included, only small periods of time can be covered. Yet this precisely was the claim that was coming to be made. Here, for example, is an assertion of it by Virginia Woolf taken from *The Common Reader*, in which she sets forth her literary creed with great vigour and charm.

Mrs. Woolf has been speaking of Montaigne, for whom she has a great admiration, and defending him from the charge of concerning himself with only trivialities.

'It is life,' she says, 'that emerges more and more clearly as these essays reach not their end, but their suspension in full career. It is life that becomes more and more absorbing as death draws near, one's self, one's soul, every fact of existence: that one wears silk stockings summer and winter; puts water in one's wine; has one's hair cut after dinner; must have glass to drink from; has never worn spectacles; has a loud voice; carries a switch in one's hand; bites one's tongue; fidgets with one's feet; is apt to scratch one's ears; likes meat to be high; rubs one's teeth with a napkin (thank God, they are good!); must have curtains to one's bed; and, what is rather curious, began to like radishes, then disliked them, and now likes them again. No fact is too little to let slip through one's fingers, and besides the interest of facts themselves there is the strange power we have of changing facts by the force of the imagination.'[1]

She then proceeds to define the distinctive quality of writers like Joyce as the attempt to come closer to life by recording 'the atoms as they fall upon the mind in the order in which they fall, by tracing the pattern, however disconnected and incoherent in appearance, which each sight or incident scores upon the consciousness'.[2]

[1] Virginia Woolf. *The Common Reader*, p. 95.
[2] *ibid*, p. 190.

H

In pursuance of this principle writers begin to describe in infinite detail the minutiae of daily life. A meticulous realism is one of the characteristic features of James Joyce's great work *Ulysses*. Joyce had already in *A Portrait of the Artist as a Young Man* shown himself a whole-hearted disciple of the 'put-everything-in' school. As an example of this method may be cited a scene from this earlier work, in which a number of students are carrying on a desultory discussion on drink, women, religious faith and the ancestors of their friends. In the middle of the discussion there occurs the following sentence: 'Cranly dislodged a figseed from his teeth on the point of his rude toothpick and gazed at it intently.' The whole of the subsequent conversation, running into several pages, is punctuated by references to the eating, chewing and spitting out of unwanted pieces of fig by Cranly.

It may well be asked why these references to the fig should be thought significant. Joyce, I conceive, is seeking to present the concrete moment of experience in all its richness, to describe not only what was happening, but *all* of what was happening. Cranly's mind was occupied with an abstract discussion, but his hand was also occupied with the dislodgement of a figseed. The second fact occurs just as truly as the first, and, since it occurs, it is from the novelist's point of view on all fours with any other occurrence. It is neither more important nor less, for whatever happens is important, and, it is apparently implied, equally important.

The implied suggestion becomes explicit in *Ulysses*. There are long passages in this book which can have no *raison d'être* except on the supposition that the novelist thinks it his business faithfully to record all incidents—even the least significant.

Take this for example: 'On the boil sure enough: a plume of steam from the spout. He scalded and rinsed the teapot and put in four full spoons of tea, tilting the kettle then to let water flow in. Having set it to draw, he took off the kettle and crushed the pan flat on the live

coals and watched the lump of butter slide and melt.'
Or again, to quote higher flights, as Mr. Gerald Gould
calls them: 'Bald deaf Pat brought quite flat pad ink.
Pat set with ink pen quite flat pad. Pat took plate dish
knife fork. Pat went.'

The defects of the method are obvious. This wealth of
non-significant detail is apt to be dull. Moreover, the
desired end of all inclusiveness can never be achieved.
The following criticism from Mr. Gerald Gould's book
The English Novel, puts the point admirably, and I quote
verbatim.

'Mr. Joyce goes from length to length, and is as far off
as ever from getting everything in. *Ulysses*, I am told,
is supposed to represent the acts, thoughts, and emotions
of a single man in a single day—though there are epi-
sodes which appear to make the scope of it wider than
that. But, if it were as huge as twenty-four telephone
directories, it could not register the acts, thoughts and
emotions which make up, for every single one of us, any
single hour of the twenty-four. The telephone directory
is, because of its rigorous selection and repression, a work
of art compared to the wastepaper basket. And *Ulysses*
is a wastepaper basket.'[1]

(3) *The Inner Life.*

Moreover—and this brings us to the next phase—not
only are people's actions occurring; there are also their
thoughts. If there is justification for a realism which
records with precision exactly what they are doing, there
is justification for recording with equal precision exactly
what they are thinking. Inevitably, then, the novel is
found to concern itself increasingly with the contents of
people's minds, and long passages are devoted to the
psychological minutiae of reverie and day dream. Here
again the development takes place in accordance with
a deliberate policy. The active life, it is pointed out, is
not the only life; it is not even the most important. What

[1] Gerald Gould. *The English Novel*, pp. 20-21.

really matters is the inner life of thought and feeling. Hence the true subject matter of the novelist is the stuff of psychology.

The following passage from Virginia Woolf, a criticism of Arnold Bennett on the ground that in concerning himself with externals he lets the stuff of life slip through his fingers, expresses this point of view.

'He can make a book so well constructed and solid in its craftsmanship that it is difficult for the most exacting of critics to see through what chink or crevice decay can creep in. There is not so much as a draught between the frames of the windows, or a crack in the boards. And yet —if life should refuse to live there? That is a risk which the creator of *The Old Wives' Tale*, George Cannon, Edwin Clayhanger, and hosts of other figures, may well claim to have surmounted. His characters live abundantly, even unexpectedly, but it remains to ask how do they live, and what do they live for? More and more they seem to us, deserting even the well-built villa in the Five Towns, to spend their time in some softly padded first-class railway carriage, pressing bells and buttons innumerable; and the destiny to which they travel so luxuriously becomes more and more unquestionably an eternity of bliss spent in the very best hotel in Brighton.'[1]

Life, it is implied, is not to be found in the mansions of Mr. Bennett, and this not because of any lack of craft, but because his conception of fiction is not such as to entrap it.

In contradistinction to Mr. Bennett's method we are told that the novelist should seek to record the inner life of thought and feeling. Yet this is exceedingly difficult, for the inner life is exasperatingly elusive. How elusive, only those who have tried to catch and pin it down can say. To illustrate the point Mrs. Woolf elaborates the view already suggested in the essay on Montaigne. The soul, she points out, is the strangest creature in the world, far from heroic, variable as a weathercock, 'bashful,

[1] Virginia Woolf. *The Common Reader*, p. 186.

insolent; chaste, lustful; prating, silent; laborious, delicate; ingenious, heavy; melancholic, pleasant; lying,
true; knowing, ignorant; liberal, covetous, and prodigal'
—in short, so complex, so indefinite, corresponding so little
to the version which does duty for her in public that a
man might spend his life merely in trying to run her to
earth. The passage in inverted commas quoted by Mrs.
Woolf is from Montaigne and serves as a text for an essay
on the theme of the changing feel and quality of life.

She bids us 'examine for a moment an ordinary mind
on an ordinary day. The mind receives a myriad impressions—trivial, fantastic, evanescent, or engraved
with the sharpness of steel. From all sides they come, an
incessant shower of innumerable atoms; and as they
fall, as they shape themselves into the life of Monday or
Tuesday, the accent falls differently from of old; the
moment of importance came not here but there. . . .'
'Life,' she continues, 'is not a series of gig lamps sym-
metrically arranged; life is a luminous halo, a semi-
transparent envelope surrounding us from the beginning
of consciousness to the end.' 'Is it not,' she concludes,
'the task of the novelist to convey this varying, this unknown and uncircumscribed spirit, whatever aberration
or complexity it may display, with as little mixture of
the alien and external as possible?'[1]

And in order to do full justice to the 'aberration and
complexity' of mental life, novelists have felt themselves
obliged to give their readers the complete contents of a
mind at a given moment. The whole higgledy-piggledy
of what, if Mrs. Woolf is right, a mind is, is presented
raw without selection or emphasis. Mrs. Woolf has herself
attempted the method with sucess, but in the hands of
lesser writers it tends to produce meaningless nonsense.
Here, for example, is a recent example in this *genre*.

'But pass the whisky. London, circling moonlight. The
most tempestuous, wreathing, writhing fabulations come

[1] Virginia Woolf. *The Common Reader*, p. 189.

from imps in bottles with hypnotic powers. A Djinn for a Jean. Go to, you would have marred all with unbridge-ability. The earth has bubbles; these are the last of them. Thank your stars for bubbles and your bubbles for stars. Bubbles in your bedroom, bubbles in your hair, bubbles on the L.G.O.C. red covered-deckers'. Hackney and Islington, Wormwood Scrubs, Victoria, and a show of Seven Kings, Commercial Road to Barking, London Bridge, Apollinaris, Cochran—all unbridgeable, but bubbling now behind a rigid hand. . . .'[1]

Or, take this from Mr. Lionel Britton's *Hunger and Love*.

'Five minutes late! Seven days' notice. Like drowning a kitten. "I'll take that bridge, if it costs a hundred thousand men! One night of Paris. They're used to it. Crippen? Go and have a look round inside St. Paul's, at the monuments".'

These reflections are recorded, presumably, in defer-ence to the conception that every psychical occurrence has significance. As with events in the outside world, so with events in the life of the mind, they are, it is thought, interesting merely because they happen.

But this is emphatically not the case. The unre-strained, unorganised movements of the mind are like dreams. People who tell their dreams are a public nuis-ance, and the psychical lives of these characters in a novel, interesting, perhaps, to the persons who experience them, interesting even to the novelist who records them, are to the reader simply boring.

(4) *The Psychological Moment.*

It is to the perception of this difficulty that the next stage in the development is due. This consists in the affirmation that the truth about life is to be found neither

[1] Out of charity I refrain from giving the author's name.

in a biography, nor in the contents of a mind, nor in its development, nor even in a psychological mood, but in a psychological moment. For—and here modern psychology makes itself felt—an individual is not, when you examine him, a personality at all; he is merely a succession of fleeting persons, each of whom endures for a psychological moment. To say *tout simple* as is sometimes done, that modern psychology has disintegrated the notion of personality is to be guilty of exaggeration. It is, however, a fact that, if what is asserted by certain schools of psychology, for example by Behaviourism, is true, the notion of personality must be a figment; nor can it be doubted that the general trend of much psychological thought is hostile to the conception. The notion of personality presupposes that in addition to the stream of psychological events, thoughts, desires, wishes, hopes, which pass through a man's consciousness and constitute his moods, there is a further entity, a consciousness through which they pass. This consciousness is a continuing thing, coloured no doubt by the character of the psychological contents which pass through it, and continuously changing, but remaining nevertheless a discreet and continuing entity, which endures through all the changes which occur in and to it. This continuing consciousness constitutes the thread of the individual's personality; it is like a river which, whether running fast or slow, speeding between steep and narrow banks, or seeping into the marshes of environing flats, remains the same river. Or, to change the metaphor, consciousness as normally conceived is like the thread of a necklace along which are strung the beads of our psychological moods and states. That there should be a continuing entity of this sort is a necessary condition of personality. For consciousness is the indispensable continuing thread which, running through all our separate moods, binds them together into a whole. It is this whole that we call the 'ego' or the personality.

Denial of continuing self.

It is just this conception of personality and of consciousness which certain modern psychological theories deny. The elimination of mind in the interests of Behaviourism described in the third chapter is extended also to consciousness. Consciousness and its correlative conception of personality the Behaviourists regard as the last survival of the medieval soul, a ghost without evidence or substance. Hume had pointed out as long ago as the eighteenth century that we have no direct experience of a personality or self. If I try to introspect myself, I come upon not a person, a continuing entity, but a hoping something, a desiring something, a thinking something, a wishing something, or, in the case in question a wondering whether there is a self; I come, in other words, not upon a continuing personality, but upon a separate psychological state, not upon a necklace but upon a bead.

It is precisely this fact of which modern psychology makes use in order to dispense with the notion of consciousness. It is not denied, of course, that we are conscious of our thoughts and wishes; what is denied is that there is a separate entity consciousness, a sort of tank or reservoir into and out of which psychological events, moods, desires and so forth swim like fishes, and which, like the tank, persists even when there are no fish. That they should have the property of being conscious is regarded simply as a characteristic or quality of psychological events. Consciousness is thus not something additional to the thoughts, wishes, and so forth, of which we are normally said to be conscious.

If this analysis is correct, a personality is not a continuing entity but a series of psychological states. These are the beads; but there is no continuing thread to link the beads; the self is simply the succession of psychological events which would normally be said to belong to or be owned by the self. Nor is it only Behaviourism which suggests this view. In many quarters there is a tendency to cast doubt upon the ordinary conception of the separate and continuing 'ego', and personality tends to be defined (for example, in the writings of Earl Russell), as the series of psychological states which would normally be defined as the states of one person, if there were a person to own the states.

A celebrated analogy of Bergson's may help to illustrate the point. Take, he says, the appearance of continuous movement presented by a cinematographic film. You seem, let us say, to be looking at the picture of one continuously moving man. This appearance of continuous identity is however an illusion. What you are in fact looking at is a series of separate static photographs, each one different from the others, yet so little different that, when they pass before your eyes in rapid succession, the appearance of continuity is preserved. This series of separate but similar cinematographic men is invested with the illusion of identity and continuity by the movement of the operator's machine. Look at what is there as it really is, before, that is to say, the reel is put on to the machine, and you will see only the series of different, instantaneous photographs which constitute the reality of the moving picture. It is just this conception of a man as a series of separate cinematographic men which, backed by the authority of psychology, intrudes itself into literature. A human being is not, says the psychologist, a continuing personality; he is a series of separate psychological momentary men. Similarly life or time is not a continuous flow; it is a series of separate, successive, instantaneous moments. But, if this is so, to try to describe a human being in terms of personality is to describe a figment. 'Very well then,' says the novelist; 'to depict reality I must concern myself with the fleeting, psychological state; to represent life as it is I must concentrate on the psychological moment of experience.'

Support from Physics.

This tendency to treat experience atomistically has been reinforced by the quantum theory in physics. The movement of the electron from one orbit to another appears, as we have seen in Chapter IV, to consist of a number of jumps, but of jumps of a peculiar kind. The jumpers with whom we are ordinarily acquainted pass, although very rapidly, over the ground intervening between their point of departure and their point of landing. But the electron does not appear to pass over the intervening space between its two orbits; all that can be said is that it appears first in one place and then in another. The evidence, in fact, is in favour not so much of the view that the electron moves in jumps, as that it exists in jumps, that, in other words, it goes out of existence in one place at one time, and comes into existence in a different place at another without apparently taking the trouble to get from the one place to the other. On this view there is no such thing as a continuing electron; the electron *is* the series of separate, shifting appearances which a continuous moving electron would present, if there were one.

Now matter consists largely of electrons and the material universe consists of matter. Hence it has been suggested that the universe itself proceeds in a series of discontinuous jumps or jerks, between any two of which it literally goes out of existence. We must not, I think, take these suggestions very seriously. They are only mentioned here as extreme illustrations of a prevalent tendency, a tendency owning a number of different sources, to suggest that to exist is not to be a continuing thing which somehow endures through time and change, but to be a series of discontinuous states or conditions each of which is exceedingly like the one that came before and the one that comes after, but is yet separated from them in time and different in identity.

Repercussions in Literature.

Applied to literature the suggestion issues in the view that the purpose of the novelist, who wishes to convey the actual quality of existence, should be to concentrate upon and to capture the actual moment of it. Existence being nothing but the succession of such moments, to make them continuous by introducing connections between them is to falsify life. Connection and continuity involve the conceptions of a human being as a personality, of time as a flow and of the succession of events as forming a continuous story. Personality and plot, character and story, the ample leisurely passage of time in which the events of the nineteenth-century novel unroll themselves, find, therefore, no place in novels which illustrate this latest phase. The psychological moment being the stuff of life, the novelist seeks to convey *all* that is happening in that moment. Here, then, we reach the complete logical development of the various tendencies that have been described.

This development may be traced in three characteristic features of the modern novel. First, there are novels which are in effect nothing but series of isolated, disconnected scenes, between which no continuity is apparent or attempted. Secondly, there is a tendency to present the scene as itself consisting of a number of isolated incidents related only by the fact of their spatio-temporal connection. Thirdly, there are experiments in style devoted to the elaboration of a new mode of writing, the headline style, consisting of a series of separate, disconnected announcements to illustrate the disconnected jumps in the thoughts and emotions of the persons who are being presented.

(i) *Novels as successions of scenes.* As an example of the first tendency may be cited the succession of scenes that constitute the movement of Virginia Woolf's *Jacob's Room*. Jacob is a baby in Cornwall; Jacob is a boy in Scarborough; Jacob is at school, at Cambridge, on a boat near the Scilly Isles, and so on. Each scene is isolated, detached; there is no hint of the time that passes between them; sometimes there is no means of ascertaining where the scene is laid, so that it is necessary to read two or three pages before discovering that one is no longer with

Professor Huxtable reading in his study, but in the school sanatorium, in London, in the Scilly Isles, or talking to half a dozen undergraduates in a college room. Sometimes the scenes presented are of considerable length; sometimes they are conveyed in a sentence or a couple of words. Consider this for example.

'Tears made all the dahlias in her garden undulate in red waves and flashed the glass house in her eyes, and spangled the kitchen with bright knives, and made Mrs. Jarvis, the rector's wife, think at church, while the hymn-tune played and Mrs. Flanders bent low over her little boys' heads, that marriage is a fortress and widows stray solitary in the open fields, picking up stones, gleaning a few golden straws, lonely, unprotected, poor creatures. Mrs. Flanders had been a widow these two years.

'"Ja-cob! Ja-cob!" Archer shouted.

'"Scarborough," Mrs. Flanders wrote on the envelope, and dashed a bold line beneath; it was her native town; the hub of the universe.'

Or this:

'At this moment there shook out into the air a wavering, quavering, doleful lamentation which seemed to lack strength to unfold itself, and yet flagged on; at the sound of which doors in back streets burst sullenly open; workmen stumped forth.

'Florinda was sick.

'Mrs. Durrant, sleepless as usual, scored a mark by the side of certain lines in the *Inferno*.

'Clara slept buried in her pillows; on her dressing-table dishevelled roses and a pair of long white gloves.

'Still wearing the conical white hat of a pierrot, Florinda was sick.'

The incidents, Archer shouting for Jacob, Florinda being sick, are apparently inserted for no reason except that they happen simultaneously with the other events recorded. Take a slice of life at a given moment, and all these things will be found happening in it. 'Very well, then,' the argument seems to run, 'put them all in for of just such disconnected happenings does life consist.'

(ii) *And scenes as successions of incidents.* As an example of the second, here is a single scene in a teashop, also from *Jacob's Room.*

'She spent tenpence on lunch.

'"Dear, miss, she's left her umbrella," grumbled the mottled woman in the glass box near the door at the Express Dairy Company's shop.

'"Perhaps I'll catch her," answered Milly Edwards, the waitress with the pale plaits of hair; and she dashed through the door.

'"No good," she said, coming back a moment later with Fanny's cheap umbrella. She put her hand to her plaits.

'"Oh, that door!" grumbled the cashier.

'Her hands were cased in black mittens, and the finger-tips that drew in the paper slips were swollen as sausages.

'"Pie and greens for one. Large coffee and crumpets. Eggs on toast. Two fruit cakes."

'Thus the sharp voices of the waitresses snapped. The lunchers heard their orders repeated with approval; saw the next table served with anticipation. Their own eggs on toast were at last delivered. Their eyes strayed no more.

'Damp cubes of pastry fell into mouths opened like triangular bags.

'Nelly Jenkinson, the typist, crumbled her cake indifferently enough. Every time the door opened she looked up. What did she expect to see?

'The coal merchant read the *Telegraph* without stopping, missed the saucer, and, feeling abstractedly, put the cup down on the tablecloth.

'"Did you ever hear the like of that for impertinence?"' Mrs. Parsons wound up, brushing the crumbs from her furs.

'"Hot milk and scone for one. Pot of tea. Roll and butter," cried the waitresses.

'The door opened and shut.'

Brilliantly observed, the separate items recorded are nevertheless unrelated. They are happenings in the same place at the same time; but beyond the spatio-temporal connection there is no other. Life is like that, Mrs. Woolf might have replied,[1] if charged with presenting a fragmentary version of it. And that life is like that nobody will want to deny. The only questions that may legitimately be raised are, why, if life is only like that, it should be recorded, and whether life is not sometimes, perhaps always, rather more than that.

(iii) *Writing in headlines*. The headline style may be illustrated from the works of any of the exponents of the psychological novel, from Virginia Woolf, from D. H. Lawrence, James Joyce or Gertrude Stein. I take as an example another quotation from Mr. Lionel Britton's *Hunger and Love*:

'Evening. Closing time. Pinch a sheet of brown paper and piece of string from packing counter.

'Morning. Opening time. In public lavatory with neat brown paper parcel.'

Or consider the following three sentences which close a chapter, each of them being given a paragraph to itself.

'Civilisation stood.

'Trade went on.

'Love resumed its sway.'

(5) *Determinism in literature*.

Two further effects of modern psychological theory

---

[1] Mrs. Woolf died in the spring of 1941.

remain to be noted. The tendency of both, like that of psychology itself, is deterministic. The first represents human consciousness as a register, a pointer-reading as Eddington would call it, of unconscious forces; the second represents human life as the plaything of external circumstance and the human spirit as the plaything of the human body. The first illustrates the influence of psycho-analysis; the second of Behaviourism.

(i) *Lawrence and Determination by the Unconscious*. The novelist who may be taken as chiefly exemplifying the first tendency is D. H. Lawrence. Lawrence was a novelist of genius who was also a novelist with a message. He had a very definite conception of life as it should be lived, with which he was perpetually contrasting life as it was in fact lived to the disadvantage of the latter. His theory of life as it should be lived was strongly influenced by the works of Freud. Indeed, it is not too much to say that it was formed by Freud. It was from Freud that it derived its two dominant principles: first, that the sources of human conduct, thought and feeling are in the unconscious; secondly, that these sources are predominantly sexual in character.

Lawrence conceives of the unconscious as a sort of underground prisoner who has become unhealthy through being kept underground. Normally he is successfully restrained by the inhibitions of social life, but every now and then at moments of excitement and especially of sexual excitement, he breaks out and comes into the open, where he shouts very loudly and very indiscreetly to the scandal of the neighbours. Most people like to think that they are gay dogs at heart and only restrained from an orgy of primitive passion and licence by the iron strength of their wills. Hence, the literary expression of this view of the unconscious has been a source of satisfaction to many well-behaved people, and has compensated them for the quiet dullness of their lives.

Lawrence, however, would not have shared his readers' pride in the strength of their self-control. His view is that the suppression and renunciation of instinctive satisfactions which society demands of human beings are bad for them, and that men's lives would be happier and freer if the unconscious, instead of being kept a cabined prisoner withheld from the light, were given free access to consciousness.

Thus he censures modern society for its hypocrisy, emphasises the force of the primitive instincts which society seeks to ignore, and represents people as swayed at moments of crisis by those very forces whose existence at the bidding of society they have denied. Lawrence thus inaugurates a new return to the primitive; he extols the natural man and derides the system of social conventions which seeks to turn him into an artificial one on the ground that it lowers vitality and is inimical to instinctive happiness.

The influence of these beliefs is continually present in his works. They are in the main records of the self-development which is for the most part the sex development of their characters. These are represented as in process of being continually swept off their feet by the violence of impulses whose existence they had never suspected; or, placed in situations to which one kind of feeling is socially appropriate, they astonish themselves and their readers by expressing the opposite feeling. Lovers, for example, who ought to be loving, unaccountably begin hating, the transition from the one emotion to the other being as apparently causeless as it is abrupt. Here for example is a typical Lawrence passage, from *Aaron's Rod*, describing the feelings of a young wife in love.

'She could never understand whence arose in her, almost from the first days of marriage with him, her terrible paroxysms of hatred for him. She was in love with him: ah heaven, how maddeningly she was in love with him: a certain unseizable beauty that was his, and which fascinated her as a snake a bird. But in revulsion, how she hated him! How she abhorred him! How she despised and shuddered at him! He seemed a horrible thing to her.

'. . . She made his life a hell for him. . . .'

Violence of lovers.

The young woman finds herself hating when she ought to love, hating when she does in fact love, as the result of an uprush of violent impulses from the unconscious which she is unable to check. The unconscious, as Lawrence portrays it, is violent, savage, primeval. The unconscious personality, like that of a child or an animal, claims all for itself, rides roughshod over others, insists on its own way. Hence, when it outcrops into consciousness, it causes a person who has been schooled to a civilised consideration for others to behave with the primitive selfishness of the spoiled child.

This primitiveness of the unconscious is chiefly manifested in the behaviour of lovers, love in Lawrence's work being an unfailing specific for its evocation. Thus his conception of the typical husband and wife is of two persons engaged in more or less perpetual struggle for mastery, each striving to dominate the personality of the other and to subdue it to his or her own.

The following is a typical passage from *The Rainbow*:

'When he sat on his perch glancing sharply round with solitary pride, pride eminent and fierce, she dashed at him and threw him from his station savagely, she goaded him from his keen dignity of a male, she harassed him from his unperturbed pride, till he was mad with rage, his light brown eyes burned with fury, they saw her now, like flames of anger they flared at her and recognised her as the enemy.'

The next quotation from *The Kangaroo*, a considerably later work, shows how this violent opposition between lovers persists throughout all Lawrence's work:

'They had another ferocious battle, Somers and Harriet; they stood opposite to one another in such fury one against the other that they nearly annihilated one another.'

It is, perhaps, beside the point to ask why, if people's unconscious selves are charged with such violent hostility to one another, they should be urged to remove the restraints with which society has endeavoured to muzzle them. That the outcropping unconscious should cause people to behave intolerably to those they love is bad enough, although Lawrence may be right in supposing that it cannot be helped. But we might at least be permitted to extend to our acquaintances a consideration and to maintain in their company a reserve which it is apparently useless to expect from our lovers; if we cannot do this, society would soon be rendered impossible. Lawrence might justifiably answer that, society being what it is, he asks nothing better. This may be all very well in theory, but it is difficult to avoid the reflection that a reversion to the jungle conditions of social intercourse, which the unleashing of people's unconsciousness would provoke, would in practice be insupportably dull.

Dullness of the primitive.

The interests of civilised people are bound up not with their emotions but with their intellects; and for an obvious reason. At the level of the emotions and the appetites we are all very much alike. Contemporary human beings when hating and loving differ very little among themselves; moreover, they differ very little from human beings hating and loving in the paleolithic age. It is only at the level of the intellect that differences emerge. Whereas my reactions when hungry to a good meal, or when drunk to a beautiful woman, differ very little from those of my remote ancestors, my reactions to a metaphysical problem, a social reform, or a Bach fugue are different. They are different not only from those of my ancestors, but from those of my neighbours, different, moreover, not only quantitatively but qualitatively. For, while the workings of the mind differ qualitatively, the emotions which Lawrence chiefly recognises differ only quantitatively. It is for this reason that, in order to achieve emphasis, Lawrence is so often driven to resort to violence. Emphasis by means of violence defeats its own ends, since constant exaggeration of emphasis deprives the writer of the power of emphasising at all.

It is exaggeration of emphasis that often makes Lawrence's books as dull as the kind of society he denounces. His characters are distinguished from each other not by variety, since, as I have suggested, it is only at the higher levels of thought and spirit that variety emerges, but by the greater or less violence of their feelings. Very soon, the characters are all feeling with more or less equal violence, and the possibility of distinction disappears. And not only of distinction between the characters, but of grading in the importance of events. Characters living in a perpetual hurricane of emotion have to bawl to make themselves heard. When they are not bawling themselves, Lawrence is perpetually bawling for them. But when one has to bawl a request for the mustard, it is not easy to raise the voice when demanding help or a divorce. Thus, in a Lawrence novel all events seem to have much the same importance, and the sense of values is lost.

Blurring of sense of values.

As I said above, the purpose of this book is not criticism but exposition, and I should not have ventured so far beyond my allotted province, were it not for the fact that many of the observations just made would apply *mutatis mutandis* to psycho-analysis itself. Psycho-analysis, like its literary manifestations, tends to subordinate the more lately evolved characteristics, the reason, will and aesthetic discrimination of mankind to the elements which we share with savages and primitives. In so doing it subordinates, I will not say the higher to the lower, but the interesting to the dull. A world in which all behaved in the way in which psycho-analysts commend would not only be a violent world but a dull one, as dull as the average film in which the only recognised motive for male human action is the desire to obtain possession of the person of a pretty female.

Psycho-analysis also tends to obscure the differences between personalities, to countenance a denial of our instinctive conviction that some things are intrinsically more important than others, and to blur the sense of values. For it no work of art is great, just as for it no person is good. The former is interpreted as the sublimation of a particular kind of frustrated sexual impulse; the latter, as one whose unconscious drives predispose him to act in ways of which other people approve.

These strictures cannot be pursued or defended here; they are mentioned only to show how, in provoking commentary and criticism in almost the same terms, the literature of Lawrence and the tendencies of psycho-analysis exhibit their common origin, or rather, how directly the first reveals its origin in the second.

(ii) *Aldous Huxley and determination by the Body*. The last tendency in modern literature to which I would draw attention, as being illustrative of modern psychology, is the determinism which represents the workings of the human spirit as a function of the workings of the human body, and exhibits the behaviour of the human organism as a function of its environment. Both these types of deterministic doctrines are, as we have seen, strongly represented in modern psychology, and are more particularly exemplified in Behaviourism. Their intrusion into literature is most marked in the work of Aldous Huxley. The view that the complexion of the mind and spirit may be coloured by the state of the body is, of course, familiar enough. Men have always known that they were depressed by indigestion, and made irritable by their livers, and that an east wind gives them headaches and fits of the 'blues'. Novelists, moreover, have always made due acknowledgement in their works of this generally recognised fact. Old men from whom favours are required are approached after dinner, not before; and it is explained that Squire Beltham had the gout when he swore continuously for half an hour at Richmond Roy.

There is, however, in Huxley's work a deliberate and constant purpose to represent the body as the determiner of the spirit, which is new. Huxley, it is obvious, resents this subjection of the soul and dislikes the body which imposes it. There is a vein of asceticism running through his work which in an earlier age would have issued in the familiar conclusion that the body is wicked and should, therefore, be mortified. Asceticism is not easy in the modern world; the times are against it. Besides, Huxley has much too acute an intelligence to be impressed by the somewhat dubious arguments by which men have been persuaded to mortify their flesh. His asceticism is temperamental rather than rational. *Intellectually* he feels to the full the force of the Greek attitude to life, and under its influence nobody has urged more strongly than he, that we must give to all sides of our natures full and free development. But if this equitable recognition of the needs of human nature as a whole, this insistence on an all-round development is a necessity of the good life, it is, so far as the body is concerned, a regrettable one. If rationality forbids us to starve the flesh, we can at least hate it. Huxley, it is clear, can never forgive the body for having attached itself to the spirit, nor cease from mocking the spirit, so dignified and pretentious, for its discreditable connection with the body. He is for ever reminding us of our humiliating dependence upon matter. Whereas the Greeks sought to restrain the overweening presumption of man by threatening him with the anger of the gods, Huxley chastises him by reminding him of the anger of his body. It will, for example, decay. There is a fine passage towards the end of *Those Barren Leaves* where Cardan, an elderly epicurean, speculates on the tragedy of old age:

'The greatest tragedy of spirit is that sooner or later it succumbs to the flesh. Sooner or later every soul is stifled by the sick body; sooner or later there are no more thoughts, but only pain and vomiting and stupor. The tragedies of the spirit are mere struttings and posturings on the margin of life, and the spirit itself is only an accidental exuberance, the product of spare, vital energy, like the feathers on the head of a hoopoe or the innumerable populations of useless and foredoomed spermatozoa. The spirit has no significance; there is only the body. When it is young, the body is beautiful and strong. It grows old, its joints creak, it becomes dry and smelly; it breaks down, the life goes out of it and it rots away. However lovely the feathers on a bird's head, they perish with it; and the spirit, which is a lovelier ornament than any, perishes too. The farce is hideous, thought Mr. Cardan, and in the worst of bad taste.'

And again:

' "Death," Mr. Cardan answered. "You can't get over the fact that, at the end of everything, the flesh gets hold of the spirit and squeezes the life out of it, so that a man turns into something that's no better than a whining sick animal. And, as the flesh sickens, the spirit sickens, manifestly. Finally the flesh dies and putrefies; and the spirit presumably putrefies too. And there's an end of your omphaloskepsis, with all its byproducts, God and justice and salvation and all the rest of them." '

Humiliation by the Body.

The body is no less intrusive in the business of love; Huxley, at least, insists on intruding it, and, as if to make a mock of the fine frenzies of the amorous soul, in the most ludicrous connections. The scene between Miss Thriplow and Calamy in *Those Barren Leaves* in which, instead of making love to his bedmate, Calamy speculates on the different contexts in which his hand may be taken, noting that it is literally a different entity and as such a source of different emotions in each, may be cited as an example. Spandrell in *Point Counter Point* so hates love because of the bodily humiliations to which it subjects him, that he takes a malicious pleasure in outraging with what he regards as humiliating refinements of sensual pleasure the native reticences of those loved and, therefore, resented women who are for him the embodiment of the detested instinct. Love, in short, is defiled by the intrusion of the body; love is, therefore, humiliating and should be avoided; our bodies are, nevertheless, insistent and love cannot be avoided, which means one more black mark against the body.

The human body may, it is true, if properly stimulated, be a source of spiritual pleasure as well as of spiritual humiliation. The best form of stimulus is drink:

'The working day was over; the bar began to fill up with men in quest of spiritual relaxation. Beer flowed, spirits were measured out in little noggins, preciously. In stout, in bitter, in whisky they bought the equivalents of foreign travel and mystical ecstasy, of poetry and a week-end with Cleopatra, of big-game hunting and music.'

Such gratifications are, however, exceptional; apart from them, the general effect of the body upon the spirit is uniformly regrettable.

Death, Birth, Chance.

I have spoken of old age and love; more important than either there is death, there is birth and there is illness. In all three the body is a source of suffering and humiliation; it is also absolute. The powerful passage on the death of Everard Webley in *Point Counter Point* admirably sums up the Huxleyan attitude:

'And meanwhile, from the air, the invisible hosts of saprophytics had already begun their unresisted invasion. They would live among the dead cells, they would grow, and prodigiously multiply and in their growing and procreation all the chemical building of the body would be undone, all the intricacies and complications of its matter would be resolved, till by the time their work was finished a few pounds of carbon, a few quarts of water, some lime, a little phosphorus and sulphur, a pinch of iron and silicon, a handful of mixed salts—all scattered and recombined with the surrounding world —would be all that remained of Everard Webley's ambition to rule and his love for Elinor, of his thoughts about politics and his recollections of childhood, of his fencing and good horsemanship, of that soft strong voice and that suddenly illuminating smile, of his admiration for Mantegna, his dislike of whisky, his deliberately terrifying rages, his habit of stroking his chin, his belief in God, his incapacity to whistle a tune correctly, his unshakable determinations and his knowledge of Russian.'

Man's beginning is no less insignificant than his end:

'Something that had been a single cell, a cluster of cells, a little sac of tissue, a kind of worm, a potential fish with gills, stirred in her womb and would one day become a man—a grown man, suffering and enjoying, loving and hating, thinking, remembering, imagining. And what had been a blob of jelly within her body would invent a god and worship; what had been a kind of fish would create and, having created, would become the battleground of disputing good and evil; what had blindly lived in her as a parasitic worm would look at the stars, would listen to music, would read poetry. A thing would grow into a person, a tiny lump of stuff would become a human body, a human mind.'

In these and similar passages Huxley, not content with showing how the mind and spirit are dominated by the body, advances to the more extreme position and insists that they *are* the body. Dissolve the body, he seems to say, and nothing is left.

I give a final passage which shows the haphazard, the almost humiliating origins of such elevation as the spirit, bound as it is in ridiculous association with the shameful body, may achieve:

' "But to be sitting with you—that's really almost incredible. And it's all due to the fact that a Manchester shopkeeper had a son with tendencies to scrofula. If Reggie Wright had been normally healthy, I'd probably be cobbling shoes in Lancashire. But luckily Reggie had tubercle bacilli in his lymph-system. The doctors prescribed a country life. His father took a cottage in our village for his wife and child, and Reggie went to the village school. But his father was ambitious for Reggie. (What a disgusting little rat he was!)" Illidge remarked parenthetically. "Wanted him to go to Manchester Grammar School, later on. With a scholarship. Paid our schoolmaster to give him special coaching. I was a bright boy; the master liked me. While he was coaching Reggie, he thought he might as well coach me. Gratis, what's more. Wouldn't let my mother pay a penny. Not that she could have done so very easily, poor woman. The time came, and it was I who got the scholarship. Reggie failed." Illidge laughed. "Miserable scrofulous little squit! But I'm eternally grateful to him and the busy bacilli in his glands. But for them I'd be carrying on my uncle's cobbling business in a Lancashire village. And that's the sort of thing one's life hinges on—some absolutely absurd, million-to-one chance." '

Here, although the spirit benefits by the weakness of the body, it is doubly reminded of its bondage, doubly mocked, once by the 'bacilli in the glands' and again by brute chance. Our minds, it seems, are the playthings of our bodies, our bodies of their environment. And in either event, whether at one remove or two, our minds are the reflection of their environment. Everybody who has read Mrs. Woolf's *A Room of One's Own* will remember the celebrated account of a luncheon party, at which a whole train of thought is changed and another set going by the spectacle of a Manx cat. And the Manx cat is observed only because there is no ash-tray:

'If by good luck there had been an ash-tray handy, if one had not knocked the ash out of the window in default, if things had been a little different from what they were, one would not have seen, presumably, a cat without a tail. . . .'

But one does see it, and presently the sight of the cat leads to the poetry of Tennyson and of Christina Rossetti. By such things, Mrs. Woolf seems to say, is our mental life, the life that we so fondly imagine to be free, determined.

It is not suggested that the above examples constitute an exhaustive survey of the effect of contemporary psychological theory upon contemporary literature; still less do they purport to give an adequate treatment of contemporary literature as such. They will, however, serve to show the extent to which theories current in the modern world, and derived mainly from psychologists, have invaded literature and affected both the methods and the matter of novelists.

BIBLIOGRAPHY

I append a short list of books which may be consulted with advantage by those who wish to pursue the various subjects touched upon in the foregoing pages. The list is divided according to chapters, the books which appear under each chapter number relating specifically to the subject matter of the chapter in question.

CHAPTER I
Joad, C. E. M. *Return to Philosophy. Philosophy for Our Times.*

CHAPTER II
Lange, F. A. *The History of Materialism.*
Cohen, Chapman. *Materialism Restated.*
Haldane, J. B. S. *The Causes of Evolution.*
Hogben, L. *The Nature of Living Matter.*

CHAPTER III
Watson, J. B. *Behaviourism.*
Pavlov, I. P. *Lectures on Conditioned Reflexes.*
Stout, G. F. *Mind and Matter.*
Huxley, Aldous. *Brave New World.*

CHAPTER IV
Eddington, Sir A. S. *The Nature of the Physical World. New Pathways in Science. Science and the Unseen World.*
Jeans, Sir J. *The New Background of Science. The Mysterious Universe.*
Levy, H. *The Universe of Science.*
Joad, C. E. M. *Philosophical Aspect of Modern Science.*

CHAPTER V
Bergson, H. *Creative Evolution.*
Haldane, J. S. *The Philosophical Basis of Biology.*
Morgan, J. Lloyd. *Emergent Evolution.*

Smuts, J. S. *Holism and Evolution*.
Broad, C. D. *The Mind and Its Place in Nature* (Section A).

CHAPTER VI

Butler, Samuel. *Evolution Old and New*.
Shaw, G. B. *Back to Methuselah*.
Joad, C. E. M. *Matter, Life and Value*.
Needham, J. *The Sceptical Biologist*.

CHAPTER VII

Myers, F. W. H. *Human Personality and its Survival of Bodily Death*.
Lodge, Sir Oliver. *Raymond*.
Price, H. *Leaves from a Psychist's Notebook. Confessions of a Ghost Hunter*.
Dunne, J. W. *An Experiment with Time*.
Moberly and Jourdain. *An Adventure*.
Geley, G. *From the Unconscious to the Conscious*.

CHAPTER VIII

Freud, S. *The Interpretation of Dreams. Introductory Lectures on Psycho-Analysis. Civilization and its Discontents*.
Adler, A. *Understanding Human Nature*.
Jung, C. G. *Psychological Types*.
McDougall, W. *An Outline of Psychology*.
Lippmann, W. *A Preface to Morals*.

CHAPTER IX

Woolf, V. *The Common Reader. To the Lighthouse. The Waves*.
Joyce, J. *Ulysses. A Portrait of the Artist as a Young Man*.
Lawrence, D. H. *Aaron's Rod. The Plumed Serpent*.
Huxley, Aldous. *Those Barren Leaves. Point Counter Point*.
Richardson, Dorothy. *Pilgrimage* (any one of the eleven volumes).
Aiken, Conrad. *Blue Voyage* (useful as an example, albeit an extreme one, of the influence of psycho-analysis on some modern novelists).

INDEX